Fresh & Fabulous
Painted
Furniture

Fresh & Fabulous
Painted
Furniture

Sterling Publishing Co., Inc. New York
A Sterling / Chapelle Book

Chapelle, Ltd.:
- Owner: Jo Packham
- Editor: Laura Best
- Staff: Marie Barber, Ann Bear, Areta Bingham, Kass Burchett, Rebecca Christensen, Brenda Doncouse, Dana Durney, Marilyn Goff, Holly Hollingsworth, Susan Jorgensen, Barbara Milburn, Linda Orton, Karmen Quinney, Leslie Ridenour, Cindy Stoeckl, Gina Swapp

Plaid Enterprises:
- Editor: Mickey Baskett
- Staff: Sylvia Carroll, Jeff Herr, Laney McClure, Dianne Miller, Jerry Mucklow, Phyllis Mueller

If you have any questions or comments, please contact:
Chapelle, Ltd., Inc., P.O. Box 9252, Ogden, UT 84409
(801) 621-2777 • (801) 621-2788 Fax • chapelle@chapelleltd.com

Library of Congress Cataloging-in-Publication Data

Fresh & fabulous painted furniture / Plaid.
        p. cm.
    "A Sterling/Chapelle book."
    Includes index.
    ISBN 0-8069-7793-0
    1. Furniture painting. 2. Stencil work. I. Plaid Enterprises.

TT199.4 .F74 2000
745.7–dc21   99-055370

10 9 8 7 6 5 4 3 2 1

Published by Sterling Publishing Company, Inc.
387 Park Avenue South, New York, NY 10016
©2000 by Chapelle Ltd.
Distributed in Canada by Sterling Publishing
c/o Canadian Manda Group, One Atlantic Avenue, Suite 105
Toronto, Ontario, Canada M6K 3E7
Distributed in Great Britain and Europe by Cassell PLC
Wellington House, 125 Strand, London WCR2 0BB, England
Distributed in Australia by Capricorn Link (Australia) Pty Ltd.
P.O. Box 6651, Baulkham Hills, Business Centre, NSW 2153, Australia
Printed in China
All Rights Reserved

Sterling ISBN 0-8069-7793-0

Table of Contents

Introduction

Today's furniture market is experiencing a renaissance in painting techniques and artistic embellishment. Not only does painted furniture add creativity to the look of a room, but also, a personal, handcrafted touch that sets it apart from other, mass-produced pieces.

With the availability of do-it-yourself kits and painting supplies in arts and crafts stores, as well as the ease of the latest techniques, there is no reason not to have a one-of-a-kind painted furniture piece in your home.

Whether you enjoy stenciling, stamping, block printing, decorative painting, or découpaging, you will find 25 projects covering all of these techniques in this book.

These projects range from a trellised magnolia room screen or a garden-themed bathroom blooming with flowers, to a romantic writing desk.

Each project comes with step-by-step instructions, patterns, and worksheets when needed, and clear color photographs. Each chapter provides detailed lists of supplies and products to use, as well as how-to photographs and instructions on the mechanics of each technique.

You will find that with the proper tools and supplies and the guidance of *Fresh & Fabulous Painted Furniture*, it is easy to create beautiful painted furniture no matter what your skill level.

Furniture Preparation

Preparing New Wood Furniture

Sand new wood furniture to remove nicks and smooth rough areas. Use 120-grit sandpaper until surface appears dusty and smooth, then use 220-grit sandpaper to finish. Sand with the grain. To round sharp edges for a worn look, use a coarse-grade sandpaper to knock down sharp corners; finish with a fine-grade.

On some new, unfinished furniture, the factory may have allowed a small amount of glue to seep out from the joints. It is important to remove this dried glue if furniture is to be stained or finished with transparent color, or area will not accept finish. Sand away all glue or scrape glue lightly with a putty knife.

When sanding between coats of paint, primer, or varnish, check surface for smoothness. If surface appears to be scratched after sanding, you are either using sandpaper or

steel wool that is too coarse, or you are sanding surface before paint, primer, or varnish is completely dry. If this happens, use a finer grit sandpaper and/or let surface dry and sand again.

Using a tack cloth, wipe away dust after sanding. (A damp cloth raises the grain of the wood.) Use a bristle brush, vacuum, or blow on the area to remove dust from crevices and corners. Finish project as desired.

Preparing Old Furniture for Staining

Using a chemical stripper, strip away old paint or varnish, following manufacturer's instructions. Use a paint scraper to remove paint, varnish, or waste and use newspapers to soak up waste. Work with the grain of the wood.

After most of old finish has been removed,

rub surface with coarse steel wool to remove more finish (again, working with grain of wood). Use a ceramic cleaning tool to scrape tight or carved areas. When surface is dry, sand smooth and wipe away dust.

If applying antiquing, glazing, or a color wash, use fine sandpaper or steel wool to prepare the surface. Work in long smooth strokes, because antiquing or color wash will pick up the direction of sanding and will show after it dries.

Using a tack cloth, wipe away dust. (A damp cloth raises the grain of the wood.) Use a bristle brush, vacuum, or blow on area to remove dust from crevices and corners. Stain project, following manufacturer's instructions.

Preparing Old Furniture for Painting

It may not be necessary to completely strip furniture before painting—sand first with a fine-grade sandpaper or steel wool to remove most of the varnish.

If furniture has been painted with oil-based paint or has layers of old paint, it is not necessary to strip piece before applying another layer of paint. Use 120-grit sandpaper until surface appears dusty and smooth, then use 220-grit sandpaper to finish. When sanding an old, painted surface, change sandpaper often due to paint buildup which occurs on paper.

If furniture is going to be painted with a light color over an already dark finish, first apply a coat of white spray primer. The primer seals the wood and prevents any dark areas of wood from showing through a light-colored base coat. It also prevents any knotholes from bleeding through months later. You should not be able to see the dark areas or knotholes after priming. If you do, apply another coat of primer in these areas.

DO NOT USE PRIMER if project is to be stained, glazed, pickled, or given a painted faux finish which involves distressing after painting.

After primer is dry, sand surface with 220-grit sandpaper, working with the grain of the wood. Wipe away dust.

Filling Holes

Fill nail holes, cracks, or gaps where sections of wood meet, with a neutral color of stainable latex filler. Using a small palette knife, apply as little as possible to fill problem area. Remove any excess while wet. Let dry, then sand smooth. If area appears sunken after drying, repeat with a second application to level out. Sand again when dry.

Applying the Base Coat

Apply base coat by brushing paint with grain of wood. Let dry. Sand surface with 220-grit sandpaper, sanding with grain of wood. Using a tack cloth, wipe away dust.

Apply a second coat of base color. Let dry. If a third coat of paint is needed, sand and wipe away dust as before. Sanding between coats of paint smooths raised wood grain and gives the surface better tooth for the next coat of paint.

Tracing & Transferring Patterns
Pattern Method #1 - Using the pattern sheet

Patterns for projects in this book are located on pages surrounding the project's instructions. To keep pattern pages intact, trace designs onto tracing paper. Transfer designs onto project surface, using transfer paper and a stylus.

Pattern Method #2 - Sketching the pattern

Sketch design on item with a chalk pencil or soapstone, using project photo or pattern as a guide.

Marking Borders

When painting a border around an object, measure and mark a continuous line with soapstone before transferring pattern to keep pattern straight.

Furniture Preparation Supplies

Primers to Use

Acrylic-based gesso gives an opaque surface preparation to prime surfaces that are free of wax and oil. It is brushed, rolled, or sponged on. Gesso can be used to coat surfaces that are not white so that the surface color of the project, such as papîer maché, will not interfere with the brightness of the base-coat color. When applied with a coarse brush or palette knife, gesso can also be used to create texture on a smooth surface.

Primer for nonporous surfaces prepares surfaces, such as glass, sealed ceramics, or metal, to give the surface a proper tooth for painting. Glass and tile medium can be painted onto glass, tile, and other slick surfaces under the area to be decoratively painted to prepare the surface for painting. Metal surfaces, such as raw tin, can be sprayed with matte acrylic sealer to prepare them for painting.

Primer for porous surfaces prepares surfaces that, if left unprimed, would absorb too much paint. It can also be used to coat project surfaces where the surface color would interfere with the brightness of the base-coat color. Primer can be brushed or rolled on.

Sandpaper, fine-grit (#120), is used to sand the surface of wood projects before basecoating. Fine-grit wet/dry sandpaper (#220) is used to sand dry base coats between applications.

Sponge brushes are used for applying base coat evenly on project surface before decorative painting is applied.

Stylus is a pencil-like tool used to transfer a traced design onto a prepared surface. A pencil or a ballpoint pen that no longer writes may also be used.

Tack cloth is used for removing sanding dust. Tack the surface after every sanding.

Tracing paper is used for tracing a design or pattern. Choose a tracing paper that is as transparent as possible for carefully tracing designs. Place tracing paper over design or pattern sheet. Secure with low-tack masking tape. With a permanent marking pen or pencil, trace main lines of pattern.

Transfer paper is used to transfer a traced design or pattern to the project surface. Choose transfer paper that has a water-soluble coating in a color that will be visible on the base-coat color of the project surface. Position the design on the project surface. Secure with low-tack masking tape. Slip the transfer paper, velvet side down, between the tracing and the project surface. Use a stylus to retrace the pattern lines, using enough pressure to transfer the lines but not so much that you indent the surface.

Wood filler is used to fill holes in wood. Apply wood filler with a putty knife. Be certain it is thoroughly dry, then sand to a smooth finish.

Finishing Supplies

Choose sealers that are nonyellowing and quick-drying. Aerosol sealers are convenient and available in gloss or matte finishes. If project is too shiny after finish coats are dry, buff with a fine-grade steel wool or water-moistened 400-grit sandpaper.

On painted surfaces, spray the dry, completed project with a coat of sealer. Let dry. Spray a second coat and let dry. Sand surface with wet 400-grit sandpaper, or with a fine-grade steel wool. Wipe away all dust. If needed, apply a third finish coat or more.

If project is made of new wood and was stained or glazed, the wood is rather porous. Therefore the surface will soak up most of the first coat of finish, requiring more coats than a painted surface.

A piece that will receive a lot of use or will be used outdoors will need more finish coats for protection.

Acrylic sealer gives a soft, matte finish that protects your painting without changing its appearance.

Outdoor varnishes give maximum durability for outdoor projects. They brush on, dry clear, and are available in gloss, satin, and matte finishes.

Artist's varnishes are specially designed for decorative artists. These clear, nonyellowing varnishes brush on in thin, even layers for greater control and elimination of brush strokes, and are available in gloss, satin, or matte finishes.

Spray acrylic sealers protect projects for use indoors. They spray on with no yellowing and are available in a lacquer-like high-gloss finish, a subtle glossy sheen, or a soft matte finish.

9

Stenciling

While the art of stenciling has always been popular for furniture and home decor, it is now easier than ever for the stenciling novice to create unlimited looks, ranging from the most simplistic borders to intricate and elegant scenes. In this chapter, we will show just how easy stenciling is with the right paints and tools. You will also learn about the different kinds of stencils available in today's crafts market and which types best meet the needs of your individual project and skill level.

Stenciling Supplies

Paints to Use

Acrylic craft paints can be used to produce opaque or soft, translucent stencil prints. These premixed, richly pigmented, and water-based paints are available in a huge array of beautiful colors, including some metallics. These paints are thinner than gel paints so care needs to be taken with technique so that bleed-unders will not occur. Clean stencils, brushes, and spills with soap and water.

Stencil dry-brush paints ensure stenciling success on any surface. They are creamy, solid paints packaged in wide-mouth, palm-size jars. Their strong, rich colors move smoothly on any surface and eliminate runs, smudges, or paint buildup on the stencil or brush. Designed for beginning stencilers, they are also used by professional stencilers because they make shading and color blending so easy.

Stencil gel paints are semitranslucent stenciling paints that offer maximum control and blending ability. They are formulated to enhance the intricate detail of stenciling, especially when shading designs. The transparent colors blend with ease to give depth to every design. They are water-based and fast-drying. The thicker gel formula prevents runs and does not leave hard edges of paint build-up. Stencil gel paints are also available in a wide variety of colors.

Glazing medium is a translucent faux-finishing, block-printing, and stamping medium that also can be used for stenciling. It is available in an array of colors, which can be mixed with neutral glaze to achieve a wide range of tones, or it can be used straight from the jar for a more opaque look. Its slower drying time also makes it easy to control.

Indoor/outdoor acrylic paints are weather resistant and very durable. They are available in a wide array of colors and provide an opaque finish which does not need to be sealed. Use brush-on, acrylic-based paints. These work in technique like acrylic craft paints. These are great for garden furniture or other pieces that get a lot of use.

Brushes, Rollers & Sponges to Use

A variety of applicators can be used for stenciling. Choose quality tools that can be used again and again.

Daubers are applicators with round sponge tips. The wooden–handled daubers are available in several widths and are ideal for painting in tight areas.

Sea sponges, slightly moistened, instantly create texture and blend colors. They are particularly effective on stencils with large openings in the design.

Sponge brushes are sponges on short wooden handles, which fit comfortably in your palm and can be reused when wet. These sponge brushes can be used with stencil dry-brush paints, acrylic craft paints, or stencil gel paints, and are available in several widths.

Stencil brushes have densely packed natural bristles for smooth, soft blending. They come in several sizes, ranging from ¼" to 2" widths. The size to choose will depend on the size of openings in the stencil. Have several of each size so that as you change paint colors, you do not have to continually wash the brush. To achieve quality stencil prints, let brushes dry thoroughly after cleaning and before using again.

Stencil rollers made from sponge are specially designed with tapered ends to prevent paint ridges. They are ideal for achieving a quick background print, or for stenciling large areas.

Stencils to Use

Stencils are cut from durable, translucent material that can be used again and again and washed clean with soap and water.

Background stencils make it quick and easy to create overall, repeating patterns that add texture and interest to surfaces. They can be used alone or in combination with other stencils.

Border, corner, and medallion stencils are single-overlay, laser-cut stencils used for exacting detail. Because they contain motifs for borders, corner motifs, and medallions, they can be arranged for limitless looks on walls, floors, and furniture.

Laser-cut stencils are multi-overlay stencils with exquisite design detail. The areas are painted in stages involving multiple stencil sheets. Each overlay contains only part of the design. These overlays are usually divided up by color. Because of the technology involved, smaller cut-out areas are possible.

Multi-overlay stencils are precut with one overlay per color. Design registration marks on each sheet make it easy to align overlays for professional-looking results. Some multi-overlay wall stencils have coordinating spot motif stencils that are perfectly sized for stenciling decorative accessories.

Mural stencils include a versatile selection of architectural and garden designs. They can be used alone, or in combination to create a one-of-a-kind mural.

Single-overlay stencils have bridges to separate different areas of the design as well as hold the stencil together. The cut-out areas as they appear on the stencil are the entire design. More than one color can be used on each design by simply taping over areas of the design when stenciling each color.

Miscellaneous Supplies & Tools

Artist's paintbrushes—rounds and flats, for enhancing stencil designs for a hand-painted look.

Chalk pencil—for marking surfaces.

Eraser—for removing slight smudges or lightening a too dark print. (Do not use a pencil eraser—it will permanently mark the painted surface.)

Liquid brush cleanser—for cleaning brushes and stencils.

Low-tack masking tape—to secure the stencil to surfaces.

Palette knife or craft sticks—for mixing and stirring paints.

Palette or disposable foam plates—for holding and mixing paints.

Paper towels—for cleaning and blotting, use a good quality towel that does not shred.

Plastic grocery bag or trash can liner—for soiled paper towels.

Plastic level—combines a ruler and level in one tool, and the plastic will not mark the wall.

Practice paper—for making paper proofs. Computer paper, poster board, shelf paper, and freezer paper (use the unwaxed side) are suitable. If you first paint the paper with the background color, you can test the design with the colors that will surround the print.

Pull-up, premoistened wipes—for whisking smudges off the furniture and cleaning hands while working.

Ruler or yardstick—for measuring.

Tack cloth—for wiping dust or lint off the surface before stenciling.

Transparent cellophane tape—for repairing stencils.

13

Brush Care & Cleanup

Thoroughly clean brushes and rollers at the end of each session. If this is not possible, wrap tools in a moist paper towel and place in a plastic bag until you can clean them.

For Brushes

Dip tips of bristles in a liquid brush cleanser. To activate cleanser, dip brush in water. Avoid soaking a stencil brush in water.

Work brush on the scrubber in the lid of the brush cleanser container. Add more water if needed to make a foamy lather. Rinse clean with running water. Blot brush on a towel to remove as much water as possible.

On larger brushes, loop a rubber band around bristle tips and roll it to the ends of the bristles to ensure that bristles do not splay. Place brushes on their sides to dry. When thoroughly dry, store brushes flat or on the handle ends with bristles up. Brushes must be completely dry before reuse.

For Sponge Rollers & Sponge Tools

Wash tools with mild soap and water. Rinse thoroughly until the water runs clean. (The sponge may be stained by paint, so you cannot tell if it is clean by looking at it.) Let dry. When the tool is damp-dry, it can be reloaded and used again.

Be certain to thoroughly clean tools at the end of the stenciling day. If paint hardens in them, it is virtually impossible to restore. While stenciling, keep tools from drying out by placing them in a zip-top plastic bag.

Stencil Care & Cleanup

Gently remove all tape before cleaning stencils. Clean according to the type of paint used.

For Acrylic Craft Paints, Stencil Gel Paints, or Glazing Mediums

Place stencil in bottom of sink. Using stencil brush, brush on a liquid brush cleanser to gently remove paint. If acrylic craft paint has dried, dip brush in rubbing alcohol to soften and remove paint. Remove dried stencil gel paints or glazing mediums by applying oil soap and gently rubbing with a pot-scrubber sponge. Rinse clean with water.

For Stencil Dry-brush Paints

Wipe stencil with a paper towel immediately after stenciling. Brush on a liquid brush cleanser. Rinse, then dry.

If the stencil dry-brush paint was not wiped off the stencil, soak stencils in strong solution of oil soap, wipe with a pot-scrubber sponge. Rinse, then dry.

Storing Stencils

After cleaning, store stencils flat in the package they came in or in large envelopes or file folders.

Repairing Stencils

If a stencil tears, repair it by applying a small amount of transparent tape to both sides of the tear. Use a utility knife to cut away tape from inside of the cut-out areas of the design.

How to Apply Liquid Paints & Gels

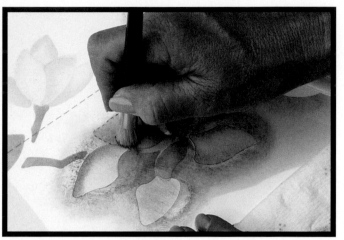

1 Squeeze out a small amount of gel or liquid acrylic paint on palette. Holding brush perpendicular to the palette, pull bristles through paint and swirl to concentrate paint in center of brush.

3 Bring paint into cut-out area with a light pouncing or circular stroke. Use more pressure on outside edge for a shaded print or use firm pressure over entire cut-out area to create an opaque print.

2 Remove excess liquid paint or gel by pouncing and swirling loaded brush on a paper towel. Begin stenciling by working brush on an uncut part of the stencil beside the cut-out area.

4 Finished stenciled Magnolia Blossoms.

How to Apply Dry Brush Stencil Paints

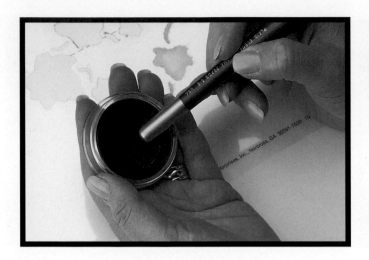

1 Remove protective coating that seals top of the paint. To remove it, use a paper towel or the handle of a stencil brush to scrape off the seal; then discard.

3 Circle loaded brush on uncut part of stencil to disperse paint. Remove any clumps of paint from stencil or brush with a paper towel.

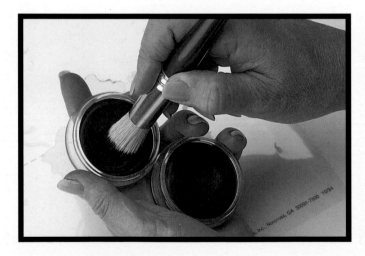

2 Holding brush as you would a pencil, circle surface of paint three or four times.

4 Stencil, using a light circular stroke. Swirl paint on entire cut-out area. Add more pressure to brush, not more paint, continuing with a clockwise then counter-clockwise stroke.

How to Apply Paint with a Roller

1 Squeeze paint on palette. Spread paint across palette with a palette knife.

3 With stencil taped in place, roll back and forth, applying even pressure. Roll in several directions, distributing paints to edges of stencil. A roller can be used with several paint colors in the same color family without cleaning.

2 Moisten roller with water and towel-dry. Roll roller through paints, distributing paint so roller is evenly covered.

4 Finished stenciled pots.

17

How to Apply Paint with a Sponge

1 Moisten sponge and pat dry. Squeeze paint onto palette. Pounce sponge into paint to load. To create a multicolored, mottled texture, pounce in several colors of stencil paint.

2 Blot excess paint on sponge by pouncing onto a clean section of the palette. Then lightly pounce sponge over cut-out area of stencil, going back over outer edge for definition.

How to Create Backgrounds

1 Mix glazing medium with neutral glazing medium to achieve a desired tint. Pour mixture onto palette. Dampen face of mitt, wring out excess water, and blot with a towel. With mitt on your hand, pat face of mitt in glaze and pounce mitt on surface to create texture.

2 Wait a few minutes for glaze to set up so it will not smear on back of stencil. Lift stencil to reveal textured print.

Glass Tabletop
Instructions begin
on page 20

Glass Tabletop

Pictured on page 19

Designed by
Kathi Malarchuk Bailey

GATHER THESE SUPPLIES

Stenciling Surface:
Glass tabletop, 36"

Stencil Gel Paints:
Spanish Moss

Brush:
Stencil brush

Stencils:
Multi-overlay stencil:
   Floral Spray

Other Supplies:
Low-tack masking tape
Matte acrylic sealer

INSTRUCTIONS

Prepare:
1. Be certain tabletop is clean and free from dirt and oil. Let dry. Referring to Furniture Preparation on pages 6–9, prepare tabletop.

Stencil the Design:
1. Using masking tape, secure Floral Spray stencil on reverse side of tabletop. Using stencil brush, stencil design with Spanish Moss.

2. Allow paint to cure for 72 hours.

Finish:
1. Apply matte acrylic sealer to tabletop.

Sunflower Chair

Pictured on page 21

GATHER THESE SUPPLIES

Stenciling Surface:
Old chair

Indoor/Outdoor Acrylic Gloss Enamels:
Antique White
Real Burgundy

Brushes:
Stencil brushes, (one per color)

Stencil:
Single-overlay:
   Welcome Sunflower

Other Supplies:
Low-tack masking tape

INSTRUCTIONS

Prepare:
1. Be certain chair is clean and free from dirt and oil. Let dry. Referring to Furniture Preparation on pages 6–9, prepare chair.

Stencil the Design:
1. Using masking tape, secure Welcome Sunflower stencil to center of chair slat. Using stencil brush, paint petals of a single sunflower in center of each slat with Antique White.

2. Stencil centers with Real Burgundy.

Finish:
1. No finish is needed for this project.

Sunflower
Chair

Instructions begin
on page 20

Checks & Vines
Table & Wall Border

Pictured on page 23

Designed by
Kathi Malarchuk Bailey

GATHER THESE SUPPLIES

Stenciling Surfaces:
Unfinished wood console
  table
Walls already painted with off-
  white, eggshell finish, latex
  paint

Acrylic Craft Paint:
Blue Ribbon

Latex Wall Paint:
Taffy

Stencil Gel Paints:
Blue Blazer
Dark Sapphire
Wedgwood Blue
Wild Ivy

Glazing Mediums:
Lemon Yellow
Mushroom
Neutral

Brushes:
Sponge brushes, 1"
Stencil brushes, (one per color)

Stencils:
Single overlay:
  Checkerboard
  Spring Vines

Other Supplies:
Chalk pencil
Level
Low-tack masking tape
Matte acrylic sealer
Sea sponge
Tape measure

INSTRUCTIONS

Prepare Table:
1. Be certain table is clean and free from dirt and oil. Let dry. Referring to Furniture Preparation on pages 6–9, prepare table.

2. Using sponge brush, base-coat entire table with 2–3 coats of Taffy. Let dry.

3. Paint front and sides of table with Blue Ribbon. Let dry.

Prepare Wall:
1. Mix Lemon Yellow and Neutral. Using damp sea sponge, sponge entire wall with mixture. Let dry for 10–15 minutes.

2. Mix Mushroom and Neutral. Using a circular motion, sponge wall with this mixture blending in a little Lemon Yellow. Let dry overnight.

Stencil Table:
1. Using masking tape, secure Checkerboard stencil on tabletop. Using stencil brush, stencil checkerboard with Wedgwood Blue. Let dry.

2. Stencil Spring Vines with Blue Blazer, Dark Sapphire, and Wild Ivy on top, legs, and front lip of table. Let dry 2–3 hours.

Stencil Wall:
1. Using tape measure and chalk pencil, mark line horizontally 36" up from floor. Using level, make certain line is accurately horizontal.

2. Referring to the photo on page 23 for placement and colors, stencil Spring Vines with Blue Blazer, Dark Sapphire, and Wild Ivy.

Finish:
1. Apply matte acrylic sealer to table.

22

Checks & Vines
Table & Wall Border
Instructions begin
on page 22

Bed of Roses
Headboard & Wall Border

Pictured on page 25

GATHER THESE SUPPLIES

Stenciling Surfaces:
Walls already painted warm
  white at top and crimson
  below the white chair rail
Headboard already painted
  soft pink with molding at top
  painted darker pink

Latex Wall Paint:
Crimson

Stencil Gel Paints:
Berry Red
Fern
Juniper
Wood Rose

Glazing Medium:
Neutral

Brushes:
Stencil brushes, (one per color)
Nylon brush, 2"

Stencil:
Laser-cut stencil:
  Blooming Rose

Other Supplies:
Low-tack masking tape
Matte acrylic sealer

INSTRUCTIONS

Prepare:
1. Be certain headboard and
wall are clean and free from
dirt and oil. Let dry. Referring
to Furniture Preparation on
pages 6–9, prepare head-
board.

2. Combine Crimson with
Neutral. Using nylon brush,
brush gently over painted
headboard to antique. Let dry.

3. Apply matte acrylic sealer to
headboard.

Stencil the Design:
1. Using masking tape, secure
Blooming Rose stencil to
surface. Using stencil brushes,
paint rose design around wall,
above chair rail, and across
headboard. Use Wood Rose
for the lighter color and Berry
Red for the darker overlay.

2. Stencil stems and leaves
with Fern and shade with
Juniper.

Finish:
1. Apply matte acrylic sealer to
headboard.

Bed of Roses Additional Colorways
Experiment with your favorite colors by stenciling the design on paper
first in order to achieve the desired results.

Tonal
  Using 2" stencil brushes, stencil each overlay
with Shadow Gray. Then, while each overlay is
in place, add Tempest Blue to shade.

Pastel
  Using 2" stencil brushes, stencil the blooms
of each overlay with Daffodil Yellow. Then,
while each overlay is in place, add Pumpkin to
shade. Stencil leaves and stems with Spanish
Moss and shade with Village Green.

Bed of Roses
Headboard & Wall
Border
Instructions begin
on page 24

Hydrangeas Bathroom

Pictured on page 27

GATHER THESE SUPPLIES

Stenciling Surface:
White porcelain bathtub

Indoor/Outdoor Paints:
Damask Blue
Eggplant
Fairway Green
Green Mist
Ink Blue
Lilac

Brushes:
Stencil brushes, (one per color)

Stencils:
Multi-overlay stencil:
 Hydrangea

Other Supplies:
Low-tack masking tape
Matte acrylic sealer

INSTRUCTIONS

Prepare:
1. Be certain tub is clean and free from dirt and oil. Let dry. Referring to Furniture Preparation on pages 6–9, prepare tub.

Stencil the Design:
1. Using masking tape, secure Hydrangea stencil to outside of tub. Using stencil brushes, stencil blossoms with Damask Blue, Eggplant, Ink Blue, and Lilac.

2. Stencil leaves and stems with Green Mist and shade with Fairway Green.

Finish:
1. Apply matte acrylic sealer to tub.

Hydrangeas Bathroom Additional Colorways
Experiment with your favorite colors by stenciling the design on paper first in order to achieve the desired results.

Tonal
 Using 2" stencil brushes, stencil blossoms, alternating with Ivory Lace and Russet.

Pastel
 Using 2" stencil brushes, stencil blossoms, with Cactus, Daffodil Yellow, and Wild Ivy. Stencil leaves and stems with Green Mist. Shade with Fairway Green.

Hydrangeas
Bathroom

Instructions begin
on page 26

Stamping

Nothing could be easier or more fun than stamping and we will show you how in this chapter. Used alone or in combination with faux finishes and stencils, stamps create beautiful, bold looks on furniture. Available in a wide variety of motifs, stamps can help pull together a room's theme decor or simply add a hint of whimsy to an interesting piece.

Stamping Supplies

Stamps to Use

Flexible stamps made from a dense, pliable material are just right for stamping on a variety of surfaces. Attached handles make positioning and lifting simple. They are available individually in a variety of designs as well as coordinated collections of stamps for creating theme designs.

Paints to Use

Acrylic craft paints can be used to produce opaque or soft, translucent stamping prints. These premixed, richly pigmented, and water-based paints are available in a huge array of beautiful colors, including some metallics.

Glazing medium is a translucent faux-finishing, block-printing, and stenciling medium that also can be used for stamping. It is available in an array of colors which can be mixed with neutral glaze to achieve a wide range of tones, or it can be used straight from the jar for a more opaque look. Its slower drying time also makes it easy to control.

Stencil gel paints are semitranslucent stenciling paints that offer maximum control and blending ability. The transparent colors blend with ease to give depth to every design. They are water-based and fast-drying. The thicker gel formula prevents runs and does not leave hard edges of paint buildup. Stencil gel paints are also available in a wide variety of colors.

Tools for Loading Stamps

Artist's flat or round brushes can be used for loading paint onto a stamp.

Sponge applicators are dense sponge wedges. They provide maximum control and are easy to clean and reuse.

Sponge brushes are round sponges on wooden handles that can be used for loading paint onto a stamp.

Sponge rollers are convenient, lightweight sponges attached to roller handles. They are ideal for large projects and frequent color changes.

Miscellaneous Supplies & Tools

Background stencils—are large stencil designs used to create an overall background pattern for stamping or to add embellishment to individual stamps.

Measurement tools—which include a spirit level, chalk pencil, ruler, and plumb line, are useful for determining the placement of stamped designs on surfaces.

Palettes or disposable foam plates—used to hold and mix paints.

Stencils—are flexible, durable patterns cut from see-through stencil plastic. Used in combination with stamps, they can add excitement to any design.

Tips for Stamping Furniture

• When marking placement guidelines on furniture, use a light chalk or charcoal pencil and keep marks to a minimum. Do not use a lead pencil—the marks are difficult to remove.

• Remove handles and hardware from furniture before stamping so they will not be in the way.

29

How to Load Stamps

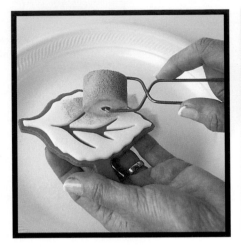

Method One: 1 Dip roller in water to moisten. Towel dry. Squeeze paint on palette. Roll roller back and forth in paint. Holding stamp in palm of hand, gently roll paint from edge to edge of stamp.

2 Load color on stamp with roller. Load another roller with a second color. Or squeeze two colors next to each other and roll roller through both colors. Do not roll so much that colors blend completely.

Method Two: Moisten sponge applicator. Blot with paper towel. Squeeze paint on palette. Dip sponge into color, then lightly pounce sponge on palette. Apply color to stamp, using light tapping, pouncing motion.

Method Three: 1 Load with brush when loading different colors on different parts of stamp. Squeeze color on palette. Dip brush in color. Lightly pounce color on stamp.

2 When using a brush, load stamp with one color, then use another brush to add second color to stamp.

Method Four: Squeeze small amount of paint on palette. Using craft knife, spread paint in thin, even coat. Place stamp face down in paint and tap lightly on back. Using handle, pick up stamp.

How to Stamp the Surface

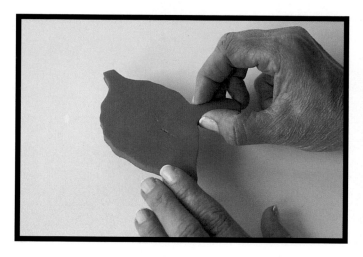

1 Hold loaded stamp by handle and position on surface. Press.

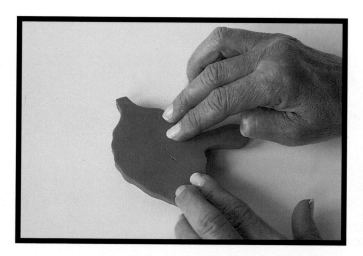

2 Release handle and gently press on back of stamp, pressing first in center of design, then on edges. Use fingers, not heel of hand, for consistent pressure in all areas.

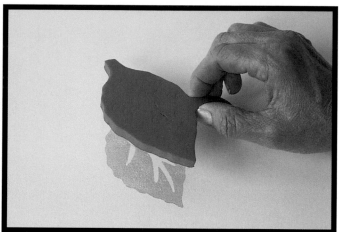

3 Using handle, lift stamp straight up off surface.

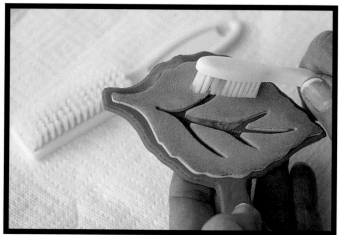

4 To clean, moisten stamp with water. Dip soft-bristle toothbrush or nailbrush in liquid soap and brush soap on top and edges of stamp. Rinse clean. Let stamp dry image side up. Store stamps loosely in a plastic bag.

Medallions
Apothecary
Chest
Instructions begin
on page 33

Medallions Apothecary Chest

Pictured on page 32

Designed by
Kathi Malarchuk Bailey

GATHER THESE SUPPLIES

Stamping Surface:
Unfinished wooden
apothecary chest

Acrylic Craft Paints:
Licorice
Napthol Crimson
Pure Gold
Wicker White

Glazing Mediums:
Black
New Gold Leaf
Pompeii Red

Brushes:
Loading brush
Sponge brushes, 1" (one per
color)

Stamps:
Medallion Collection

Other Supplies:
Low-tack masking tape
Matte acrylic sealer
Pencil
Ruler
Sandpaper, 220-grit
Tack cloth

INSTRUCTIONS

Prepare:
1. Be certain chest is clean
and free from dirt and oil. Let
dry. Referring to Furniture Preparation on pages 6–9, prepare
chest. Remove drawer pulls.

2. Using sponge brush, base-
coat chest, except drawer
fronts, with Licorice. Let dry.
Sand chest. Using tack cloth,
wipe away dust.

3. Using ruler, pencil, and
masking tape, mask off a 2½"-
wide border around top of
chest. Apply a second coat of
Licorice to chest, except
center area of top or drawer
fronts, referring to the photo
on page 32 for color placement. Let dry. Remove tape.

4. Paint inset on top of chest
and drawer fronts, except
areas that divide panels, with
two coats of Wicker White. Let
dry. Sand between coats.

5. Mask off a ¼" border around
inset on top and around each
drawer. Paint borders and
bottom rim with Pure Gold. Let
dry. Remove tape.

6. Mask off a ¼" border at front
corners. Paint edge of top and
border with Napthol Crimson.
Let dry. Remove tape.

Stamp the Design:
1. Using loading brush and
Medallion Collection stamps,
stamp large square medallion
at center of top inset and on
five drawer fronts, with Black,
referring to the photo for
placement.

2. Stamp round medallion on
remaining drawer fronts with
Pompeii Red.

3. Stamp smallest medallion in
corners of inset and around
edge of top with New Gold
Leaf.

Finish:
1. Paint four drawer pulls with
Napthol Crimson. Paint five
drawer pulls with Licorice.
Let dry.

2. Brush drawer pulls with
New Gold Leaf. Let dry.
Replace drawer pulls.

3. Apply matte acrylic sealer to
chest.

Leafy Glade Cottage Chest

Pictured on page 34

Designed by
Kathi Malarchuk Bailey

GATHER THESE SUPPLIES

Stamping Surface:
Unfinished, wooden three-
drawer chest

Glazing Mediums:
Neutral
Sage Green
White

Brushes:
Loading brush
Stencil brush

Stamps:
Leaf Collection

Stencils:
Checkerboard Collection

Other Supplies:
Low-tack masking tape
Matte acrylic sealer
Sandpaper, 220-grit
Soft cloth
Tack cloth

Continued on page 35

Leafy Glade
Cottage Chest
Instructions begin
on page 33

Continued from page 33

INSTRUCTIONS

Prepare:
1. Be certain chest is clean and free from dirt and oil. Remove drawer pulls. Referring to Furniture Preparation on pages 6–9, prepare chest.

2. Sand chest. Using tack cloth, wipe away dust.

3. Using soft cloth, apply White to chest and drawer pulls. Let dry.

4. Lightly sand. Wipe away dust. Apply a second coat of White to deepen color. Let dry.

Stamp the Design:
1. Using loading brush, apply Sage Green to Leaf Collection stamps. Stamp leaves on drawer fronts and top of chest, referring to the photo on page 34 for placement. Let dry.

2. Using masking tape, secure Checkerboard Collection stencils to sides of chest. Mix Neutral with Sage Green. Using stencil brush, stencil checks on sides of chest with mixture.

Finish:
1. Using soft cloth, apply Sage Green on drawer pulls and around top edge of chest. Let dry.

2. Apply matte acrylic sealer to chest. Let dry.

3. Replace drawer pulls.

Fern Prints

Fern Prints

Designed by
Kathi Malarchuk Bailey

GATHER THESE SUPPLIES

Stamping Surface:
Handmade paper (enough for three framed prints)

Glazing Mediums:
Deep Woods Green
Moss Green
Sage Green

Stamp:
Martha's Fern

Other Supplies:
Scissors
Wooden picture frames (3)

INSTRUCTIONS

Prepare:
1. Using scissors, cut handmade paper to fit in frames.

Stamp the Design:
1. Using Martha's Fern stamp, stamp fern fronds on pieces of handmade paper with Deep Woods Green, Moss Green, Sage Green. Let dry.

Finish:
1. Insert paper in frames.

Block Printing

Block printing has come a long way since the days of carving designs into raw potatoes. With the advent of soft, sponge shapes that can be manipulated to go around curves and over trims, ideas for creating whole decorative scenes and murals are endless. With today's blocks, you can create soft, naturalistic designs, using glazing mediums or stencil gel paints.

Preparing the Work Area

Set up a work area on a sturdy table covered with paper or plastic. Check lighting to minimize eyestrain. Be certain to read project instructions and package instructions for stencils, printing blocks, paints, and tools before beginning.

If working with many block-printing pads, have a container of water with a drop of mild dish soap nearby for cleaning the blocks.

Have brushes handy. One brush is used to load several colors of glazing medium. Swish brush in water, then blot it dry on a terry towel when changing to another color family.

Keep paints and supplies on a different table to avoid smudges.

Block-printing Supplies

Blocks to Use

Printing blocks are die-cut from a soft and durable stamping material that is easy to clean and can be used time and time again. Each block has its own handle that makes loading and setting the block onto the surface easier. Available in a wide range of precut designs, there are blocks for every decorating style, as well as blank block materials so that you can cut your own designs. Blocks are also flexible, which means you can use them on just about any surface, around corners, over molding trims, and on most rounded surfaces.

Paints to Use

Glazing mediums are rich, thick blocking mediums with a subtle transparency that re-create the shades of nature. Thanks to the gel-like consistency, each print will possess its own natural shadings. Available in a wide array of colors, glazing mediums are water-based and nontoxic.

Tools for Loading Blocks

Loading brushes are used to load blocks. The most common used is a flat artist's brush. Though one brush can be used for several colors within the same family, you should have two or three loading brushes available.

Script Liners are pointed, round artist's brushes used for the final step of adding just a hint of vines and tendrils to the block print.

Miscellaneous Supplies & Tools

Brown paper bag—for blotting loaded block.

Chalk or ¼" quilter's tape—for marking wall surface.

Disposable foam plate—for palette.

Old, terry hand towel—for drying brushes and hand cleanup.

Practice paper—for making paper proofs.

Slightly moistened hand towel—or pull-up, premoistened wipes for correcting mistakes.

Small bowl of water—for cleaning brushes and maintaining blocks.

Soft toothbrush or cellulose sponge—for cleaning blocks.

Guidelines for Designing Furniture Scenes

Choosing Colors

Spend some time deciding which colors and designs will work best in your home. Deep, rich tones such as burgundy, deep green, and deep purple work best in traditional, Victorian, or rustic homes. Clear, bright colors, pastels, and primary colors work best in modern and contemporary environments. If you are adding or refinishing a single furniture piece, choose colors that will fit with the style of the room. If you are redecorating an entire room, select a color palette that coordinates with a major element, such as floor covering or draperies, or a major piece of furniture, such as a sofa.

Measuring, Proportion & Balance

To ensure the design you have chosen will fit the furniture, measure carefully before you start. Compare measurements with the sizes of stencils and block-printing designs.

Choose designs that are the proper size. Large pieces of furniture need large motifs to "fill them up." Smaller pieces can hold one large motif and smaller motifs for balance.

Achieving balance is as important as staying in proportion. When grouping items, try to use odd numbers (like three or five) of a motif, rather than an even number of motifs.

Placement

A wonderful way to test if your imagined scene will fit the furniture piece is to first make paper proofs. Stencil or block-print the designs on large pieces of paper, cut them out, and then tape them to the furniture piece. This will allow you to check the size and placement of design motifs. It is easy to adjust the design by simply moving the proofs. Paper proofs are also a good way to check colors and to practice stenciling and shading techniques. Before removing the proofs, you can mark their placement on the furniture with chalk or light pencil. When you are ready to start, use a plumb line and/or a spirit level to be certain the placements are straight and even.

How to Block Print

1 Squeeze dime-sized amount of color on palette. Hold block by handle. With flat brush, apply thin coat of color to cut side of block extending out to edges of block.

3 Holding loaded block by the handle, place on project surface. Release handle. Gently press block against surface without sliding it. On smaller blocks, walk fingertips over surface of block. On larger blocks, press with your palm, being certain to press all edges.

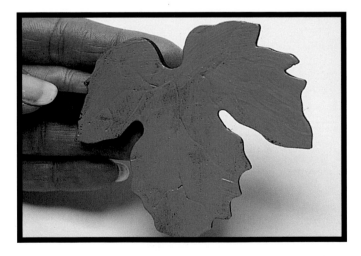

2 Completely cover block. Do not get color on handle.

4 Use handle to lift block. Move to another area and make a second press, repeating until it is necessary to reload. You can get 2–5 presses, depending on desired intensity.

Block-printing Hints

Shading—For color variations, apply more than one tone of a color to the block. Always apply the light color first. Blend colors together with the same loading brush.

Multicolor Loading—The internal cuts within the block can serve as distinct color lines. Several shades that are not within the same color family can be loaded on the block. Notice that the bird has Russet loaded on the breast, several shades of Blue on the wings and tail, and even a dot of Black for the beak and eye.

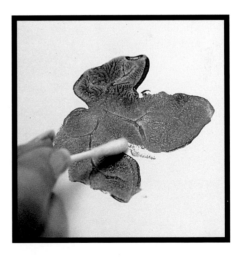

Blotting—To prevent smudging on the first print, blot the block on a scrap of brown paper bag before setting the block. When printing a multicolor load, blotting prevents smudging.

Correcting Mistakes—remove smudges before they dry with a slightly moistened cotton swab. Then reblock in the same place.

Pressing Techniques

You should be able to get three pressings, or prints, from one load of color.

1st Print
The first press is always darker so it appears to be closer. Block printing is greatly enhanced with this type of shading.

Shadowing
To make a shape appear as if it is behind another, use the following procedure: When the darker print (which will appear closer) is dry, stack another leaf or shape behind by pressing the top portion of the shape; roll the bottom of the shape off the surface and press the top portion only up to the edge of the first print.

2nd Print
The second print is the pressing that most people prefer.

Half-printing
This printing technique works well with most leaf shapes. It gives the illusion of a leaf with a portion turned up or a side view of a leaf. With a block that is ready for the second or third pressing, gently roll the leaf in half and press the rolled leaf against the side of another leaf (be certain the first leaf print has dried).

3rd Print
The third pressing can add still more depth to the print.

Cutting Your Own Printing Block

1 Choose a simple, silhouette-type design. Trace design with sharp lead pencil onto tracing vellum. You can also use actual leaves or flowers by pressing them and placing them on a copy machine to reduce or enlarge as desired. Trace design onto tracing vellum. In either case, make certain you add a handle to design.

　　To cut outer edge, place printing block material on glass. Place pattern over printing block material and secure with tape. Use a sharp craft knife to cut through pattern into pad.

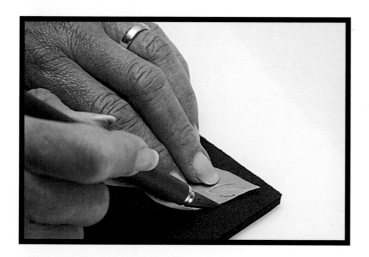

2 On straight edges, make a clean, straight cut all the way through pad. Keep side of blade flush against pattern. Do not angle blade. Achieve a straight up-and-down cut. On curved edges, use a sawing motion to cut about half-way through at the points and turns, lift blade and reposition it. Do not try to rotate material with blade in position.

3 To cut veins and details, hold pattern to surface and cut through tracing. Cut halfway through printing block material, following detail markings. Be careful not to cut completely through pad. Remove tracing.

　　Test block before working on actual project. If there are ragged edges, put a new blade into craft knife and carefully trim ragged edges away.

Geranium Garden Bench

Designed by
Kathi Malarchuk Bailey

GATHER THESE SUPPLIES

Block-printing Surface:
Cedar bench

Glazing Mediums:
Deep Woods Green
Geranium Red
Ivy Green
Pompeii Red

Stencil Gel Paints:
Ivory Lace
Twig
White

Brushes:
Flat, #4
Script liner
Stencil brushes, (one per
    color)

Printing Block:
Geraniums

Stencils:
Pots & Planters

Other Supplies:
Low-tack masking tape
Water-based polyurethane,
    matte finish

INSTRUCTIONS

Prepare:
1. Be certain bench is clean and free from dirt and oil. Let dry. Referring to Furniture Preparation on pages 6–9, prepare bench.

Stencil the Design:
1. Using masking tape, secure Pots & Planters stencil on bench. Using stencil brush, stencil pots with Ivory Lace.

2. Using #4 flat brush, shade pots with Twig, and highlight with White.

Block-print Design:
1. Using Geranium printing blocks, block-print geranium flower petals with Geranium Red and Pompeii Red.

2. Block-print leaves around flowers and pots with Deep Woods Green and Ivy Green.

3. Using script liner, paint stems and tendrils with Ivy Green.

4. Using stencil brush, pounce Ivy Green around tops of pots to simulate moss. Let dry 72 hours.

Finish:
1. Apply 3–4 coats of polyurethane to bench.

Geranium
Garden Bench

Garden Window Armoire

Pictured on page 45

Designed by
Kathi Malarchuk Bailey

GATHER THESE SUPPLIES

Block-printing Surface:
Unfinished wooden armoire

Acrylic Craft Paint:
Midnight

Glazing Mediums:
Bark Brown
Deep Purple
Deep Woods Green
Ivy Green
Lilac
New Leaf Green

Latex Wall Paint:
Off-white

Stencil Dry-brush Paint:
Terra Cotta

Stencil Gel Paints:
Ivory Lace
Russet
Tempest Blue
Twig
Wedgwood Blue

Brushes:
Flat, #4
Script liner
Sponge brushes, 2"
Stencil brushes, (one per color)
Stencil roller

Printing Blocks:
Ivy set
Lilac & Hydrangeas set

Stencils:
Bricks & Cobblestones
Pots & Planters
Window

Other Supplies:
Low-tack masking tape
Palette or disposable plates
Sandpaper, 220-grit
Sea sponge
Water-based polyurethane,
  matte finish

INSTRUCTIONS

Prepare:
1. Be certain armoire is clean and free from dirt and oil. Let dry. Referring to Furniture Preparation on pages 6–9, prepare armoire.

2. Using sponge brush, base-coat armoire with 2–3 coats Off-white. Let dry. Sand between coats. Let dry.

3. Dampen sea sponge. Squeeze excess water from sponge. Pour a small amount of Bark Brown onto palette. Dip sponge in color. Lightly sponge sides, lower front, and lower doors of armoire, using a horizontal motion, to simulate siding. Let dry. Wash sponge.

4. Squeeze excess water from sponge. Pour a small amount of Wedgwood Blue onto palette. Dip sponge in color. Lightly sponge upper doors to simulate sky. Let dry.

Stencil the Design:
1. Using masking tape, mask off lower part of armoire. Using stencil roller and Bricks & Cobblestone stencil, stencil bricks on doors, front, and sides with Russet. To shade, intensify color in some areas by rerolling. Remove tape.

2. Using Window stencil, stencil windows on two upper doors, enlarging stencil to fit doors as needed. To enlarge, stencil one side, feathering stroke when approaching middle. Reposition stencil on other side and stencil, feathering toward center and blending. Use same technique for all stencil overlays. Stencil sash with Twig. Stencil frame with Tempest Blue.

3. Using sponge brush, paint molding at top and base and trim windows with Midnight.

4. Paint carved trim above upper doors with Tempest Blue.

5. Using Pots & Planters stencil, stencil planter at lower right with Terra Cotta. Stencil planter at center left with Russet.

6. Using #4 flat brush, shade planters with Twig. Stencil details with Ivory Lace.

Block-print the Design:
1. Block-print ivy leaves in planters with Deep Woods Green, Ivy Green, New Leaf Green.

2. Block-print lilac leaves with Deep Woods Green, Ivy Green, New Leaf Green.

3. Block-print lilac flowers with Deep Purple and Lilac.

4. Using script liner, paint stems and branches with diluted Bark Brown. Let dry.

Finish:
1. Apply 2–3 coats polyurethane to armoire.

Garden
Window
Armoire
Instructions
begin on
page 44

Potted Herbs Cabinet

Pictured on page 47

Designed by
Kathi Malarchuk Bailey

GATHER THESE SUPPLIES

Block-printing Surface:
Wooden cabinet with two
raised-panel doors

Antiquing Washes:
Ivy Green
Oak Brown
White

Glazing Mediums:
Deep Woods Green
Ivy Green
Lilac
New Leaf Green

Stencil Dry-brush Paints:
Terra Cotta
Truffles Brown

Printing Blocks:
Dandelion & Italian Parsley set
Sage, Mint, Chives set

Stencils:
Pots & Planters

Brushes:
Flat, #4
Script liner
Sponge brushes
Stencil brushes, (one per color)

Other Supplies:
Low-tack masking tape
Matte acrylic sealer

INSTRUCTIONS

Prepare:
1. Be certain cabinet is clean
and free from dirt and oil. Let
dry. Referring to Furniture
Preparation on pages 6–9,
prepare cabinet.

2. Using masking tape, mask
off door panels on cabinet.

3. Using sponge brush, apply
Oak Brown to top, sides, front,
and frames of doors, following
manufacturer's instructions. Let
dry. Remove tape.

4. Mask off center areas of
door panels. Apply White to
center areas of panels. Let dry.
Remove tape.

5. Mask off beveled edges
between center areas and
door frames. Apply Ivy Green.
Let dry. Remove tape.

Block-print & Stencil Design:
1. Using small pot stencil and
stencil brush, stencil a pot on
each door panel with Terra
Cotta, referring to photo for
placement.

2. Using #4 flat brush, shade
pots with Truffles Brown.

3. Block-print chives, Italian
parsley mint, and sage leaves
with Deep Woods Green, Ivy
Green, New Leaf Green.

4. Block-print chive and sage
blossoms with Lilac.

Finish:
1. Using script liner, add stems
with diluted Deep Woods
Green, Ivy Green, and New
Leaf Green. Let dry.

2. Apply matte acrylic sealer to
cabinet. *Note: If your antiquing
washes are self-sealing, you
will not need to use a sealer.*

Potted Herbs
Cabinet

Instructions begin
on page 46

Instructions begin
on page 46

Twining Ivy Wall Shelf

GATHER THESE SUPPLIES

Block-printing Surface:
Unfinished wood shelf

Glazing Mediums:
Bark Brown
Deep Woods Green
Ivy Green
Neutral
Sage Green

Latex Wall Paint:
Creamy White, satin

Brushes:
Script liner
Sponge brush, 2"

Printing Block:
Ivy

Other Supplies:
Steel wool, #0000
Tack cloth
Water-based urethane varnish

Twining Ivy
Wall Shelf

INSTRUCTIONS

Prepare:
1. Be certain shelf is clean and free from dirt and oil. Let dry. Referring to Furniture Preparation on pages 6–9, prepare shelf.

2. Using sponge brush, base-coat shelf with two coats of Creamy White. Let dry.

3. Using steel wool, lightly sand. Using tack cloth, wipe away dust.

Block-print Design:
1. Mix Neutral with the Deep Woods Green, Ivy Green, and Sage Green. Using Ivy printing blocks, block-print ivy leaves with the green glazes individually and in combination to achieve a varied, natural look.

2. Mix Bark Brown with Neutral. Using script liner, paint vines to connect the ivy leaves with mixture.

Finish:
1. Apply two coats of urethane varnish to shelf.

Decorative Painting

Nothing complements a piece of furniture more than the custom look of decorative painting, and this chapter offers something for everyone who wants to try their hand at it. Not only will you find a handy list of supplies and tools, but also pattern sheets and worksheets to help you step-by-step in your painting. No matter what your skill level, decorative painting is easy with the right tools and supplies.

Decorative Painting Supplies

Paints to Use

Acrylic craft paints are a favorite of decorative painters because of their creamy formula and long open time. These premixed, richly pigmented, and water-based paints are available in a huge array of beautiful colors.

Glazing mediums are translucent colors that enhance realistic effects. Neutral glaze can be mixed with other glaze colors and even with paint colors to create tints or more translucent paints. The glazes are perfect for sponging, stippling, and many faux-finishing techniques.

Indoor/outdoor acrylic paints are weather resistant and very durable. They are available in a wide array of colors and provide an opaque finish, which does not need to be sealed.

Metallic acrylic craft paints include finishes such as, pearl, gemstone, and metallic. They add glimmer, shine, and luster to accent the decorative painting projects.

Painting Mediums to Use

Painting mediums are added to or used along with acrylic colors to change their properties so that they can be used for specific functions, such as painting on glass, painting on fabrics, used for antiquing, etc.

Blending gel medium will make blending easier. It will keep the paints moist, giving more time to enhance your artistic expression with shading and highlights. Dampen the area on which you wish to paint with blending gel. As long as the medium stays wet, the paint will blend beautifully.

Extender, when mixed with paint, will extend drying time and add transparency when floating, blending, and washing colors. Create effects from transparent to opaque without reducing color intensity.

Floating medium simplifies one of the most difficult painting techniques. When loaded into the brush along with the paint, the color can literally be "floated" onto the surface. This technique is used for shading and highlighting. It is easier to float a color with the paint plus floating medium than with the paint plus water because you will have more control, and the floating medium will not run as water will. Simply load brush with floating medium, blot on a paper towel, then load with paint. Floating medium does not contain extenders, so it will not extend the drying time of the paint.

Glazing medium, when mixed with acrylic paint, gives the perfect consistency to a topcoat that can be combed or textured with other techniques, as well as used as an antiquing glaze. Generally, mix ⅓ glazing medium to ⅔ paint.

Thickener, when mixed with paint, creates transparent colors while maintaining a thick flow and consistency. It is also used for marbleizing and other painted faux finishes.

51

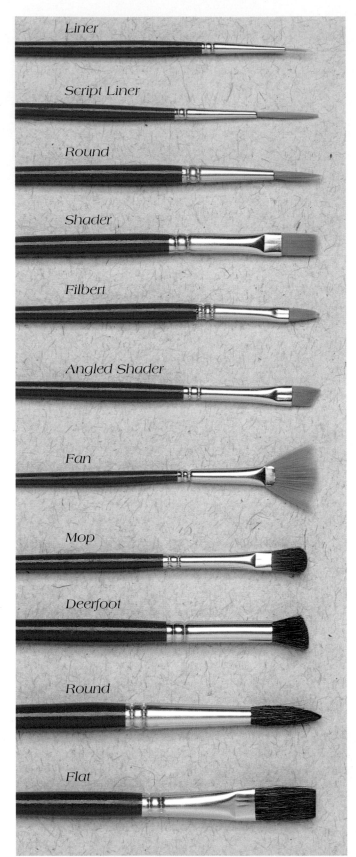

Liner

Script Liner

Round

Shader

Filbert

Angled Shader

Fan

Mop

Deerfoot

Round

Flat

Brushes to Use

The brushes you use are important tools in achieving a successful painted design, so shop for the best you can afford. The size brush you will use at any given time depends on the size area you are painting. Small designs require small brushes, and so forth. Trying to paint without the proper size brush is a major mistake.

Rectangular Brushes

Bright: Brights are rectangular in shape and have shorter hairs than flat brushes. The shorter hairs give the brush more resilience when pushing wet color onto the project surface or when pressing to removing paint from a surface. Because brights can carry a large amount of paint, they can be used for wide strokes as well as chisel-edge strokes, sharp corners, and details. The shorter hairs allow the painter to achieve textures that are not possible with other brushes.

Flat: Flat brushes are rectangular in shape, with long hairs. The chisel edge can be used to make fine lines and the flat edge can make wide strokes. Because flats have longer hair extending from the ferrule than brights, they can carry a large quantity of paint without having to reload often. Flats can be used for double-loading, side-loading, and washing.

Scruffy: Scruffy brushes are wide, rectangular brushes with short bristles similar to a bright. Scruffy brushes can be purchased or you can simply use a damaged or worn-out brush. They cannot be used for strokes, but work well for pouncing or stippling, dry-brushing, streaking, or dabbling.

Wash/Glaze: A wash/glaze brush is a large flat brush (sized in inches, i.e. ½", ¾", 1", etc.) for applying washes of color and finishes.

Round Brushes

Liner: Liner brushes are round and have shorter hairs than scrollers. These are used to paint small areas. They are often used to paint fine, flowing lines and calligraphic strokes.

Round: Round brushes have a round ferrule and the hairs taper to a fine point at the end. These brushes can be very useful in base-coating, but are also helpful with stroke work. The fine tip works well for painting details and tiny spaces.

Scroller: A scroller is a long-haired round brush used to make fine lines and scrolls. It is helpful for the paint to be thin when using this brush so it flows easily from the brush onto the project surface.

Miscellaneous Brushes

Angular: The angular, or angled, brush is a flat brush with the hairs cut at an angle. The angular brush paints a fine, chiseled edge and is perfect for painting curved strokes, sharp edges, and blending.

Deerfoot Shader: A deerfoot shader is a round brush with the hairs cut at an angle. It can be used for shading, stippling, and adding texture.

Fan Brush: A fan brush is a finishing brush that is traditionally used clean and dry. Lightly bounce the flat side of the brush on wet surfaces for textured effects. Blend the edges between wet glazes to achieve very soft gradations of color.

Filbert: A filbert is a flat brush with a curved end. Because the tip is tapered it can make very fine, chiseled lines and the rounded tip does not leave noticeable start and stop marks. It is also helpful for curved strokes, filling in, and blending.

Mop: A mop is a round brush with very soft, long hairs. It is primarily used for smoothing, softening, and blending edges.

Scroller

Scruffy

Wash/Glaze

Flat

Stencil

Stencil: A stencil brush is a round brush with either soft or stiff bristles. The paint is applied either with a pouncing motion or a round circular motion. These brushes need very little paint loaded onto them, and excess paint is dabbed off onto a paper towel before applying to the project surface.

Brush Accessories

Water container—with clean water to rest the brush in. Keep the ferrule and handle out of the water. A container with a ridged bottom helps clean the bristles.

Brush cleanser—use a liquid brush cleanser that can clean wet or dried paint from bristles, and grooms brushes between uses.

Miscellaneous Supplies & Tools

Palette—for laying out paints. You will load the brush, blend the paint into the brush, and mix colors on a palette.

Palette knife—for both mixing and applying paint. Palette knives come in two styles. Both have long, flat blades, but one type has an elevated handle to help keep your hand out of the paint. A good palette knife should be thin and flexible when it touches the project surface.

Soft cloth—for wiping away sanding dust and excess antiquing medium or glaze. It is also used for wiping brushes since rough paper towels can damage brushes.

Brush Care & Cleanup

Brushes must be properly cleaned and cared for. When you buy a good quality brush, it has sizing in it to hold the hairs in place. Before painting, remove the sizing by gently rubbing the hairs in your fingers. Then, thoroughly clean the brush with water. After you have completed the painted design, wash the brush, being careful not to abrade or abuse the hairs. Work the bristles back and forth with a brush cleanser. When you have removed the paint pigment from the brush, leave the cleanser in the brush and shape the brush with your fingers. Rinse the brush before using it to paint.

Painting Tips

Working with Acrylics

• Squeeze paint onto palette, making a puddle of paint about the size of a nickel.

• Pull color with brush from edge of puddle. Do not dip brush in center of puddle; putting too much paint on edges.

• Let each coat dry before applying a second coat. if and area is cool to the touch, it is probably still wet.

• Acrylic paints blend easily. Add white to lighten a color. Add black to darken.

Basic Painting Terms

Base-coat—is to cover an entire area with one or several initial coats of paint. Let base coat dry before continuing.

Dirty brush—contains wet color left from the last application. Wipe brush gently, pick up next color, and begin painting. There will be a hint of the previous color along with the new color.

Double-load—puts two colors on the brush that blend to make a third color at the center of the brush.

Dry-brush—to apply small amounts of paint to a dry surface. Use a round, or filbert brush. Load brush with color. Brush several times on a folded paper towel to remove almost all of the paint, then lightly stroke the design.

Float—See side-load.

Highlight—to lighten and brighten an area. Apply two to three layers of color rather than one heavy one. Highlighting on a moist surface has a soft effect; brush on a dry surface for a brighter look. If instructions call for highlighting twice, the first application should be made on a surface moistened with blending gel medium. The second application should be lightly brushed on a dry surface.

Inky—is diluting paint with water until paint is the consistency of ink.

Load—is to stroke brush back and forth in paint until brush is full.

Retard—uses an additive to extend the drying time. Use a small container to hold retarder while painting. Using a flat brush, apply over entire surface. It will not hurt the brush to keep it in retarder over extended periods.

Shade—deepens color within the design to create dimension. Apply color with a side-loaded brush on a slightly moistened surface. Shading can be applied as many times as needed to build depth and intensity of color. Let paint dry and moisten surface again before adding another layer of color.

Side-load—is used for shading and highlighting. Side-loading is also called floating.

Spatter—to speckle project. Using an old toothbrush, dip bristles into water. Blot on a paper towel to remove excess water. Dip brush into paint, working paint into bristles by tapping on palette. Point brush toward area to be spattered and pull thumb across bristles.

Stipple—by pouncing tips of brush bristles on surface to add paint. You can also stipple with a dry brush (round, filbert, or mop) to help blend color after it has been applied with a side-loaded brush. DO NOT wash brush you are using for blending paint until you are finished for the day. You cannot stipple to blend paint with a damp brush.

Tints—to add touches of color for interest and depth. Load small amount of contrasting paint on a filbert brush and apply to project. To soften color, lightly brush with mop brush to blend out.

Undercoat—is painting part of the design with white paint when painting on a dark surface, so design paint color shows.

Wash—to alter or enhance a painted design. Apply a layer of transparent color (thinned paint) over a dry base paint.

Wet-into-wet blending—using two or more colors on the brush and blending while still wet.

How to Load a Flat Brush

 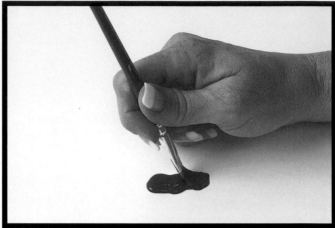

1 Hold brush at edge of puddle of paint on palette. Pull paint out from edge of puddle with brush, loading one side of brush.

2 Turn brush over and repeat to load other side. Brush back and forth on palette. Keep flipping brush and brushing back and forth on palette to fully load bristles.

How to Load a Liner

1 Squeeze a puddle of paint onto palette and dilute it at edge with water.

2 Stroke liner along edge of puddle, pulling paint into brush. Stroke brush on palette to blend paint into bristles.

How to Multiload a Scruffy Brush

1 Hold brush at edge of puddle of first color of paint on palette. Push brush straight down into puddle of first color.

3 Look at brush to see that bristles are loaded half with each color. Do not overblend to mix colors.

2 Turn brush to another area and push into edge of puddle of second color. Turn brush around and pounce onto first color again.

4 If desired, dip brush into puddle of third color.

How to Side-load

1 Load flat brush with extender. Blot off excess.

2 Touch corner of brush in paint. Lift brush and blend on palette. Color will drift softly across brush, fading into nothing on opposite side.

How to Double-load

1 Dip flat brush in floating medium. Blot off excess on paper towel until bristles lose their shine.

2 Touch one corner of brush in one paint color. Touch opposite corner of brush in another paint color. Stroke brush to blend colors at center of brush. Colors should remain unblended on corners.

Basic Brush Strokes

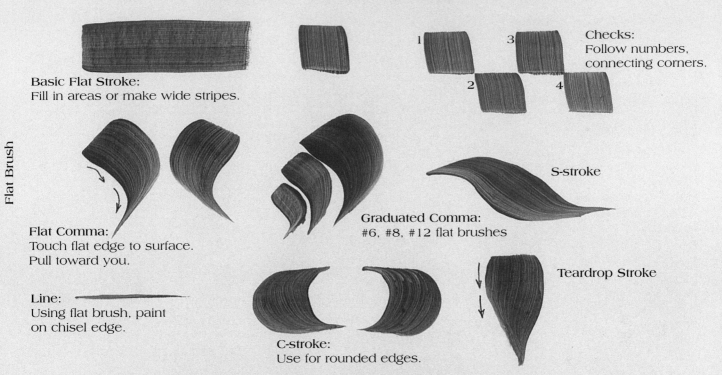

Flat Brush

Basic Flat Stroke:
Fill in areas or make wide stripes.

Checks:
Follow numbers, connecting corners.

Flat Comma:
Touch flat edge to surface. Pull toward you.

S-stroke

Graduated Comma:
#6, #8, #12 flat brushes

Teardrop Stroke

Line:
Using flat brush, paint on chisel edge.

C-stroke:
Use for rounded edges.

Round Brush

Teardrop Stroke

Comma

Violets:
Using all round brushes, make comma strokes.

Triple Stroke:
Form teardrop for center and comma strokes for sides.

Liner

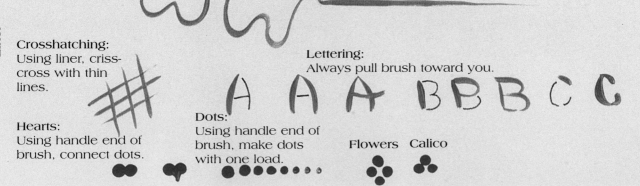

Crosshatching:
Using liner, criss-cross with thin lines.

Lettering:
Always pull brush toward you.

A A A B B B C C

Hearts:
Using handle end of brush, connect dots.

Dots:
Using handle end of brush, make dots with one load.

Flowers   **Calico**

Animal Stack Cabinet

Pictured on page 61

GATHER THESE SUPPLIES

Painting Surface:
Wooden cabinet

Acrylic Craft Paints:
Barn Wood
Burnt Umber
Country Twill
Huckleberry
Indigo
Licorice
Maple Syrup
Raspberry Wine
Tapioca
Terra Cotta
Wicker White
Wrought Iron

Glazing Medium:
Neutral

Brushes:
Flats, #4, #8
Liner, #1
Sponge brushes, 1"
Stencil brush, ½"

Other Supplies:
Antiquing medium:
    Down Home Brown
Black permanent marker
Craft knife
Matte acrylic sealer
Palette or disposable plates
Paper towels
Sandpaper, 220-grit
Spatter tool
Stencil blank material
Tack cloth
Wood stain of your choice
    (optional)

INSTRUCTIONS

Prepare:
1. Be certain cabinet is clean and free from dirt and oil. Let dry. Remove hinges and locking tab. Referring to Furniture Preparation on pages 6–9, prepare cabinet.

2. Using palette, mix a small amount of Burnt Umber into Neutral to create a stain. Using sponge brush, stain cabinet with mixture or stain it with wood stain of your choice.

3. Paint sides, front, door, legs, and locking tab with Tapioca. Let dry. Sand for a worn look. Using tack cloth, wipe away dust.

Paint the Design:
Checks:
1. Using black permanent marker, transfer Animal Stack Cabinet Pattern on page 62, onto stencil blank material. Using craft knife, cut out stencil for checks.

2. Using stencil and stencil brush, paint checks with Wrought Iron.

3. Using #4 flat brush, paint a line above and below checks with Huckleberry and Raspberry Wine.

Cows:
1. Base-coat cow with Maple Syrup. Shade with Licorice and Maple Syrup.

2. Using liner, paint spots with Tapioca.

3. Paint eyes, nostrils, and mouth with Licorice. Highlight eyes with Tapioca.

4. Paint tail with Maple Syrup. Stroke end of tail with Licorice.

Sheep:
1. Using #4 flat brush, base-coat legs with Licorice.

2. Base-coat fur with Barn Wood and a touch of Licorice.

3. Base-coat face and ears with Licorice.

4. Base-coat head with Barn Wood and a touch of Licorice.

5. Using stencil brush, pick up Tapioca, blot on a paper towel, place bristles flat on sheep, and swirl to create a woolly effect.

6. Using #8 flat brush, shade body with Licorice.

7. Highlight edges of ears with Tapioca. Paint eyes, nose, and mouth with Tapioca.

Chicken:
1. Using #4 flat brush, base-coat chicken and wing with Wicker White.

2. Using #8 flat brush, shade around chicken and wing with thinned Indigo.

3. Using #4 flat brush, base-coat comb, beak, and wattle with Terra Cotta.

4. Using #8 flat brush, shade with Huckleberry.

5. Using liner, add strokes of Wicker White to create wing and tail feathers. Using handle end of brush, dot eye with Licorice.

Continued on page 62

Animal
Stack
Cabinet
Instructions
begin on
page 60

Continued from page 60

Bird & Hearts:
1. Using #4 flat brush, base-coat bird and wing with Licorice.

2. Using #8 flat brush, highlight wing with Tapioca.

3. Paint leg with Licorice. Using handle end of brush, dot eye with Tapioca.

4. Using #4 flat brush, base-coat hearts with Huckleberry and Raspberry Wine.

5. Using #8 flat brush, shade with Huckleberry, Indigo, and Raspberry Wine.

Flag & Flagpole:
1. Base-coat flagpole with Burnt Umber. Shade ball with Licorice.

2. Using #4 flat brush, base-coat blue field with Indigo.

3. Base-coat remainder of flag with Country Twill.

4. Base-coat stripes with Huckleberry.

5. Using #8 flat brush, shade bottom with Huckleberry and Indigo. Shade at fold with Indigo.

6. Base-coat stars with Country Twill. Let dry.

Finish:
1. Using spatter tool, spatter cabinet with Licorice. Make spattering heavier at bottom and edges. Let dry.

2. Apply matte acrylic sealer to cabinet. Let dry.

3. Antique with Down Home Brown. Let dry.

4. Apply matte acrylic sealer to cabinet. Let dry.

5. Replace hinges and locking tab.

Animal Stack Cabinet Pattern

Enlarge pattern 265%

Birdhouses &
Dogwood
Potting Bench
Instructions begin
on page 64

Birdhouses & Dogwood Potting Bench

Pictured on page 63

Designed by
Chris Stokes

GATHER THESE SUPPLIES

Painting Surface:
Wooden cabinet

Acrylic Craft Paints:
Apple Spice
Blue Ribbon
Burnt Carmine
Burnt Umber
Fresh Foliage
Hauser Green Dark
Licorice
Raspberry Wine
Rose Chiffon
Slate Blue
Tapioca
Yellow Light

Latex Wall Paint:
Creamy White
Off-white

Glazing Medium:
Neutral

Brushes:
Flat, #10
Glaze, ¾"
Liner
Paint roller, 4"-wide
Rake, ¾"
Round, #5
Sponge brush, 1"
Stencil brush

Other Supplies:
Antiquing medium: Down
    Home Brown
Low-tack masking tape
Sandpaper, 220-grit

Spattering tool
Tack cloth
Transfer tools
Water-based varnish

INSTRUCTIONS

Prepare:
1. Be certain cabinet is clean and free from dirt and oil. Let dry. If a smoother finish is desired, sand surface. Using tack cloth, wipe away dust. Referring to Furniture Preparation on pages 6–9, prepare cabinet. Remove door pulls.

2. Sand main shelf of cabinet.

3. Using sponge brush, antique with Down Home Brown. Let dry.

4. Using masking tape, mask off main shelf. Using paint roller, paint remainder of cabinet with Off-white. Let dry.

5. Reroll painted areas with Creamy White. Let dry. Remove tape.

6. Mask off lower shelf, edges of doors, and edges of side panels.

7. Using palette, mix equal amounts of Hauser Green Dark and Neutral. Using sponge brush, streak glaze mixture across lower shelf, edges of doors, and edges of side panels. Let dry. Remove tape.

Mauve Birdhouse

8. Using transfer tools, transfer Birdhouse and Dogwood & Nest Patterns on page 66 onto cabinet.

Paint the Design:
Dogwood Branches & Leaves:
1. Using #5 round brush, paint branches with inky Burnt Umber and Hauser Green Dark.

2. Using #10 flat and ¾" glaze brushes, paint leaves with inky Hauser Green Dark and a touch of Burnt Umber. Just touch, press, and pull to a point. Let dry.

3. Using liner, detail leaves and twigs with inky Burnt Umber and a touch of Hauser Green Dark.

Dogwood Blossoms:
1. Load #10 flat and ¾" glaze brushes with Rose Chiffon/ Tapioca. With darker color on outer edge, paint petals.

2. Float Raspberry Wine on outer edge. (Do not forget the dip in the petals.)

3. Using liner, outline edge of dip with Burnt Carmine.

4. Using stencil brush, pounce centers of blossoms with Hauser Green Dark and a touch of Burnt Umber and Fresh Foliage.

5. Using handle end of brush, dot centers with Fresh Foliage and Tapioca.

6. Dry-brush highlights with Tapioca on petals as needed, pulling from outer edge in toward center.

Mauve Birdhouse:
1. Using glazing brush, paint walls with Apple Spice. Shade with Raspberry Wine.

2. Using #10 flat brush, paint roof with Raspberry Wine.

3. Using liner, outline with Tapioca.

4. Using #10 flat brush, float opening with Licorice.

Bird's Nest & Eggs:
1. Using ¾" rake brush, paint a wispy nest with inky Yellow Light. Pick up Burnt Umber and Licorice to shade.

2. Using liner, paint twigs with inky Tapioca and a touch of Yellow Light.

3. Using #10 flat brush, float eggs with Blue Ribbon and a touch of Tapioca.

Blue Roof Birdhouse:
1. Shade walls with Burnt Umber. Reshade with Licorice.

2. Paint perch and opening with Burnt Umber.

3. Float roof with Slate Blue. Let dry.

Finish:
1. Using spattering tool, spatter cabinet with inky Burnt Umber. Let dry.

2. Apply 2–3 coats varnish to cabinet.

Bird's Nest & Eggs

Birdhouse Patterns

Enlarge patterns 240%

Dogwood & Nest Patterns

Daisies
& Roses
Chest

Instructions
begin on
page 68

Daisies & Roses Chest

Pictured on page 67

Designed by
Phillip C. Myer &
Andy B. Jones

GATHER THESE SUPPLIES

Painting Surface:
Wooden chest of drawers

Acrylic Craft Paints:
Baby Blue
Burnt Umber
Hauser Green Dark
Hauser Green Light
Ice Blue
Light Red Oxide
Medium Yellow
Navy Blue
Titanium White
True Burgundy

Indoor/Outdoor Acrylic Paints:
Damask Blue
White

Brushes:
Flat shaders, #10, #12
Flats, #10, #16
Liner, #2
Stencil brush

Stencils:
Multi-overlay stencil:
    Canterbury Scroll

Other Supplies:
Low-tack masking tape
Palette or disposable plates
Paper towels
Pencil
Ruler
Transfer tools
Water-based varnish
White drawer pulls

INSTRUCTIONS

Prepare:
1. Be certain chest is clean and free from dirt and oil. Let dry. Remove drawer pulls. Referring to Furniture Preparation on pages 6–9, prepare chest.

2. Using #16 flat brush, base-coat chest with a mixture of Damask Blue and White. Let dry completely.

Stencil Background Design:
1. Create a lighter value of the base color by adding more White. *Tip: Save some of the base color in case touch-ups are needed.*

2. Using ruler and pencil, measure to find center point of each side and top of chest.

3. Using masking tape, secure Canterbury Scroll stencil, on one side of chest at center mark.

4. Load stencil brush with the Damask Blue and White mixture. Swirl brush on a paper towel to remove excess paint. Stencil design, applying paint in all openings. Move stencil to next area and repeat until all areas of top and sides are stenciled, including edges, referring to the photo on page 67 for placement. Let dry.

5. Using the same techniques as in Step 4, stencil the second overlay. Let dry.

Stencil design

Repeat design

Paint the Design:
Daisies:

1. Refer to Chest Center Design on page 70. Using transfer tools, trace and transfer Daisies & Roses Patterns onto chest.

2. Refer to Daisies & Roses Worksheet on page 71. Using #12 flat shader, base-coat daisy petals with Titanium White. Base-coat center with Medium Yellow.

3. Load #10 flat shader with Navy Blue. Load #12 flat shader with Baby Blue and dip into Titanium White. Paint one petal at a time, following this procedure for all petals: Place small brush stroke of Navy Blue on interior of petal. Immediately overstroke, using brush loaded with Baby Blue and Titanium White—touch brush to surface, apply pressure, pull, and drag brush up to form a tail with chisel edge of brush.

4. Reload #10 brush with Navy Blue for each petal. Wipe #12 brush on a paper towel before reloading with Baby Blue and tipping into Titanium White. Let daisies vary in color by varying amounts of Baby Blue and Titanium White.

5. Using #10 flat brush, apply another coat of Medium Yellow to the center. Let dry.

6. Shade centers with Light Red Oxide and Medium Yellow.

7. Highlight top of center with a double-loaded brush of Medium Yellow and Titanium White.

Daisies & Roses Patterns

Enlarge patterns 375%

8. Using liner, add pollen dots with thinned Burnt Umber, Light Red Oxide, Medium Yellow, and Titanium White.

Roses:
1. Refer to Daisies & Roses Worksheet on page 71. Create dark burgundy mixture of 60% True Burgundy and 40% Burnt Umber. Set mixture aside.

2. Create medium value pink with dark burgundy mixture and Titanium White.

3. Double-load #12 flat brush with medium pink and dark burgundy mixture. Blend on palette to soften colors.

4. Paint a scallop stroke at back center of the rose. Place a comma stroke on either side. This forms the back of the rose.

5. Repeat three strokes just below first ones to form second layer of back petals. Connect those petals to the bowl of the rose with a U-stroke. Make a second U-stroke just below the first one.

6. Paint side petals with comma strokes. Add smaller petals on top. Place a Lazy-S stroke in the lower center to create a petal flipping upward.

Leaves:
1. Base-coat leaves with Hauser Green Light. Apply several coats. Let dry completely. (If you rush, the paint will lift.)

2. Working one leaf at a time, apply an even coat of blending gel medium to leaf.

Chest Center Design

Double-load #10 flat brush with Hauser Green Dark and Hauser Green Light. Place dark green at base of leaf.

3. Fill in top of leaf with Hauser Green Light. Stroke to blend from the bottom of leaf to top.

4. While paint is still wet, wipe brush on a paper towel and load with Ice Blue. Stroke Ice Blue on the leaf from top edges of leaf to center.

5. Using liner, paint vein with Ice Blue. Let dry.

Finish:
1. Apply several coats of varnish to chest.

2. Install drawer pulls.

Daisies & Roses Worksheet

Using #12 flat shader, undercoat petals with Titanium White and center with Medium Yellow.

Place small brush stroke of Navy blue on interior of petal. Overstroke with Baby Blue and Titanium White.

Using #10 flat brush, shade centers with Light Red Oxide and Medium Yellow. Highlight top of center with Titanium White and Medium Yellow. Using script liner, add pollen dots with thinned Burnt Umber, Light Red Oxide, Medium Yellow, and Titanium White.

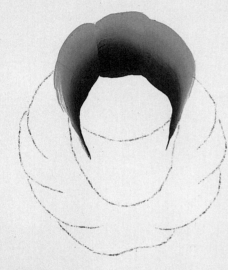

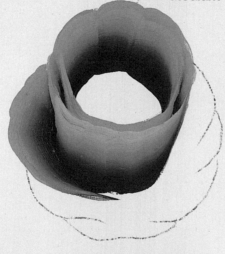

Using #12 flat brush, paint scallop stroke, then comma stroke on either side at back with burgundy mixture.

Repeat three strokes just below first ones to form second layer. Connect petals to bowl with U-stroke. Paint second U-stroke just below first one.

Paint sides of petals with comma strokes. Add smaller petals on top. Place Lazy-S stroke in lower center to create petal flipping upward.

Using #10 flat brush, paint leaf with Hauser Green Dark and Hauser Green Light.

Fill in top of leaf with Hauser Green Light. Stroke to blend from bottom of leaf to top.

Stroke on leaf from top edge of leaf to center with Ice Blue. Using liner, paint vein with Ice Blue.

Birds & Checks Table

Pictured on page 73

Designed by
Faith Rollins

GATHER THESE SUPPLIES

Painting Surface:
Table with tabletop measuring
at least 11" x 23"

Acrylic Craft Paints:
Burnt Umber
Clay Bisque
Huckleberry
Indigo
Licorice
Medium Yellow
Nutmeg
Olive Green
Raw Umber
Slate Blue
Teal Green
Thicket

Brushes:
Filbert, #6
Flat, #12
Liner
Sponge brush

Other Supplies:
Antiquing medium, Brown
Matte acrylic sealer
Palette or disposable plate
Sandpaper, 220-grit
Self-sealing stain, color of your
    choice
Spatter tool
Tack cloth
Transfer tools

INSTRUCTIONS

Prepare:

1. Be certain table is clean and free from dirt and oil. Let dry. Referring to Furniture Preparation on pages 6–9, prepare table.

2. Using sponge brush, stain tabletop with a stain color of your choice.

3. Using #12 flat brush, paint legs and lower part of table with Thicket.

4. Sand lower portion of table, removing all paint is some areas. Using tack cloth, wipe away dust.

5. Using transfer tools, transfer Birds & Checks Table Pattern on page 75 onto tabletop.

Paint the Design:
Tree Branches:
1. Using #12 flat brush, triple-load by first loading the brush with Raw Umber then dip one corner of the brush in Burnt Umber and the other corner in Nutmeg. Blend colors on palette. Paint larger branches starting with brush flat and ending up on the chisel edge.

2. Using liner, paint smaller branches with same colors used for larger branches.

3. Using #6 filbert brush, paint leaves double-loaded with Thicket and Olive Green.

4. Paint leaf stems and veins with thinned Raw Umber.

Crows:
1. Paint crows Licorice.

2. Highlight wing with Clay Bisque and Licorice.

3. Using handle end of brush, dot eye with Medium Yellow. When dry, dot with Licorice for pupil.

Tall Birdhouse:
1. Using #12 flat brush, paint tall birdhouse Slate Blue plus Teal Green.

2. Shade with a float of Indigo.

3. Paint roof with Huckleberry.

4. Form shingles on birdhouse with thinned Indigo.

Short Birdhouse:
1. Paint birdhouse Clay Bisque.

2. Shade with a float of Raw Umber.

3. Paint roof Slate Blue plus Teal Green.

4. Paint board lines with Raw Umber.

5. Indicate wood grain with thinned Raw Umber.

Both Birdhouses:
1. Paint entrance holes with Licorice.

2. Shade inside each entrance hole with thinned color of the house.

Continued on page 74

Birds & Checks Table

Instructions begin
on page 72

Continued from page 72

3. Paint perches with Licorice.

4. Shade under perches with the shading color of each house.

5. Paint hook on top of birdhouses with Licorice.

6. Paint hanging rope Licorice and Raw Umber.

7. Stencil checkerboard with Licorice, fading out checks while moving toward painted design.

Finish:
1. Using spatter tool, spatter tabletop with Licorice.

2. Apply matte acrylic sealer to tabletop.

3. Antique tabletop with antiquing medium. Wipe out highlights and darken around edges of tabletop. Let dry.

4. Apply matte acrylic sealer to tabletop.

Birds & Checks Table Pattern

Enlarge pattern 275%

Flowers & Sunshine Chest

Pictured on page 77

Designed by
Tasha Yates

GATHER THESE SUPPLIES

Painting Surface:
Wooden chest with drawer
    and open shelves

Indoor/Outdoor Acrylic Colors:
Black
Dandelion Yellow
Deep Purple
Eggshell
Lanier Blue
Pink Blush
Spring Green
White

Brushes:
Round, #3
Petit-four sponge applicator
Sponge brushes, ¾", 1", 1¾"
Stencil brush, ⅜"

Other Supplies:
Low-tack masking tape, ¾"-
    wide
Pencil
Ruler
Scissors
Transfer tools

INSTRUCTIONS

Prepare:
1. Be certain chest is clean
and free from dirt and oil. Let
dry. Remove drawer pull.
Referring to Furniture Preparation on pages 6–9, prepare
chest.

Paint the Design:
Background:
1. Using 1¾" sponge brush,
paint sides and back inside
shelf area with Eggshell.

2. Paint top of chest and
shelves with Spring Green.

3. Paint drawer with Lanier
Blue.

4. Using pencil and ruler,
measure in and mark sides
1⅞" from top and each side
and 3⅝" from bottom. Using
masking tape, mask off.

5. Using 1" sponge brush,
paint area inside tape with
Lanier Blue. Let dry.

6. Using stencil brush, paint
clouds on drawer front and on
blue areas of sides with White
in a light, swirling motion.
Remove tape. Let dry.

7. Mask off a border ¾"-wide
around blue areas on sides.
Paint border with White.
Remove tape. Let dry.

8. Using ¾" sponge brush,
paint front of chest and areas
outside border on sides with
Deep Purple. Let dry.

9. Using scissors, cut ¾"
square from petit-four sponge.
Using square sponge, paint
squares on white borders with
Continued on page 78

Heart Patch Pattern

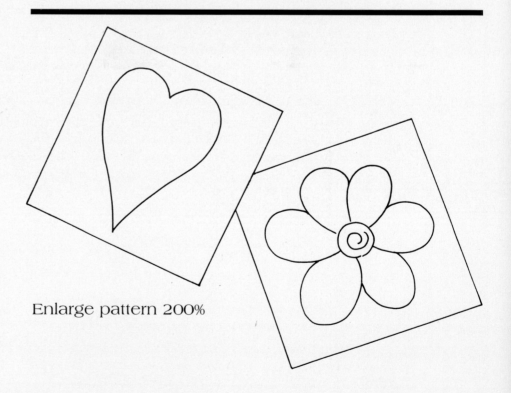

Enlarge pattern 200%

Flowers & Sunshine Chest

Instructions begin
on page 76

Continued from page 76

Black to make checkered border. Let dry.

Flowers on Sides:
1. Using transfer tools, transfer Flower Pattern onto blue areas on sides of chest.

2. Using #3 round brush, paint petals with Pink Blush.

3. Paint stems, leaves, and grass below flower with Spring Green.

4. Using 1¾" sponge brush, paint flower centers with Dandelion Yellow.

Patches on Top:
1. Transfer Heart Patch Pattern on page 76 onto top of chest.

2. Using #3 round brush, paint background of heart patch with Dandelion Yellow.

3. Paint background of flower patch with Lanier Blue.

4. Paint heart with Deep Purple.

5. Paint flower petals with Pink Blush.

6. Using ¾" sponge brush, paint center of flower with Dandelion Yellow.

7. Using handle end of brush, dot heart with Spring Green.

Patch on Shelf:
1. Transfer Heart Patch Pattern onto top of lower shelf.

2. Paint background of heart patch with Dandelion Yellow.

3. Paint heart with Lanier Blue.

4. Using handle end of brush, dot heart with Pink Blush.

Finish:

1. Using #3 round brush, paint drawer pull with Dandelion Yellow. Let dry. Install drawer pull.

2. Paint rays around pull with Dandelion Yellow.

3. Outline patchwork shapes on top and shelf and painted flowers on sides with Black. Add swirls in centers of flowers and blades of grass. Let dry.

Flower Pattern

Enlarge pattern 200%

Flowers & Sunshine Chair

Pictured on page 81

Designed by
Tasha Yates

GATHER THESE SUPPLIES

Painting Surface:
Wooden chair with spindle
  back

Indoor/Outdoor Acrylic Colors:
Black
Dandelion Yellow
Hot Rod Red
Lanier Blue
Pinwheel Blue
White

Brushes:
Liner
Shader, #6
Sponge brush, 1"
Stencil brush, ⅜"

Other Supplies:
Matte acrylic sealer
Transfer tools

INSTRUCTIONS

Prepare:
1. Be certain chair is clean and free from dirt and oil. Let dry. Referring to Furniture Preparation on pages 6–9, prepare chair.

Paint the Design:
Back:
1. Using sponge brush, paint rounded part of back with Dandelion Yellow.

2. Paint spindles with Hot Rod Red and Lanier Blue. Let dry.

3. Paint a stripe around each spindle with Black.

Legs:
1. Paint legs with Dandelion Yellow, Lanier Blue, and Pinwheel Blue. Let dry.

2. Paint a stripe around each front leg with Black.

3. Paint center supports with Lanier Blue.

4. Paint side supports with Hot Rod Red.

Seat:
1. Paint seat with Lanier Blue. Let dry.

2. Using stencil brush, paint clouds on seat with White in a light swirling motion. Let dry.

3. Using transfer tools, transfer Sun Pattern below & Lettering Pattern on page 82 onto seat.
Continued on page 82

Sun Pattern

Enlarge pattern
130%

Flowers & Sunshine Chair

Instructions begin
on page 80

Continued from page 80

4. Using #6 shader, paint sun with Dandelion Yellow. Paint rays with Dandelion Yellow.

5. Paint bee with Black, Dandelion Yellow, and White. Let dry.

6. Using liner, paint face on sun, flight line of bee, and lettering with Black. Let dry.

Finish:
1. Apply matte acrylic sealer to chair.

Lettering Pattern

Enlarge pattern 130%

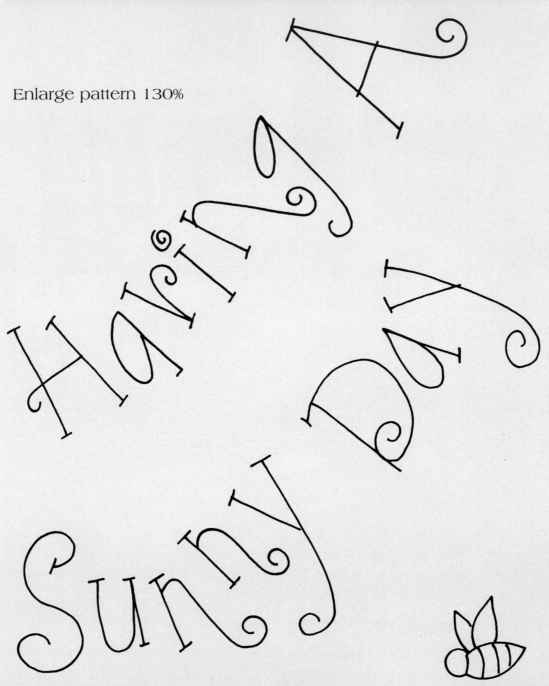

Gigi's Garden Patio Table

Pictured on page 84

Designed by
Gigi Smith-Burns

GATHER THESE SUPPLIES

Painting Surfaces:
Clay pot, 19" dia. x 16" high
Clay saucer, 19" dia.

Acrylic Craft Paints:
Aspen Green
Bayberry
Bluebell
Buttercrunch
Indigo
Lemon Custard
Lemonade
Licorice
Portrait Light
Raspberry Wine
Rose Chiffon
Slate Blue
Thicket
Warm White
Wrought Iron

Indoor/Outdoor Acrylic Paint:
Vanilla

Brushes:
Angular
Round, #3
Liner, #1
Sponge brushes, 1" (one per color)

Other Supplies:
Palette or disposable plates
Round glass tabletop, 28½" dia.
Sea sponge
Transfer tools
Water-based varnish, satin

INSTRUCTIONS

Prepare:
1. Be certain pot and saucer are clean and free from dirt and oil. Let dry. Referring to Furniture Preparation on pages 6–9, prepare pot and saucer.

2. Using a dampened sea sponge, base-coat pot and saucer by sponging with Vanilla. Let dry overnight.

3. Sponge rim and slightly below rim of large pot with Bayberry. While paint is still wet, sponge with Thicket. Let this sponging fade out as it meets the area for leaves. Sponge the same colors on rim of saucer. Let dry.

4. Using transfer tools, transfer Saucer Pattern on page 85 onto inside of saucer.

5. Transfer Pot Patterns #1–#6 on pages 91–96 onto sides of pot. (Pot will be used upside down.) When transferring pot patterns, align points B, C, D, and E together. Align point F with point A.

Painting the Design:
Irises:
1. Refer to Iris Painting Worksheet on page 87. Using sponge brush, base-coat irises with Bluebell.

2. Shade with Slate Blue. Highlight with Warm White. Reinforce previous shading with Indigo.

3. Using the corner of an angular brush, paint beards. Stipple with Raspberry Wine, Buttercrunch, and Lemonade.

Daffodils:
1. Refer to Daffodil Painting Worksheet on page 88. Base-coat with Buttercrunch.

2. Shade with Rose Chiffon. Highlight with Warm White.

3. Float around trumpet part of flower with a brush-mix of Lemon Custard and Lemonade.

4. Reinforce shading on petals with very transparent Raspberry Wine.

Tulips:
1. Base-coat with Portrait Light.

2. Shade with Rose Chiffon. Highlight with Warm White.

3. Reinforce previous shading with Raspberry Wine.

Leaves & Stems:
1. Base-coat some leaves (selected randomly) with Aspen Green. Shade with Wrought Iron.

2. Base-coat remaining leaves with Bayberry. Shade with Thicket. Highlight with Lemonade. Reinforce previous shading with Wrought Iron.

3. Load #3 round brush with Bayberry and dip it into Wrought Iron. Stroke in stems.

Dragonfly:
1. Refer to Dragonfly & Damselfly Worksheet on page 89.

2. Base-coat dragonfly with a wash of Rose Chiffon.

3. Shade with Raspberry Wine.

Continued on page 85

Gigi's Garden
Patio Table
Instructions begin on
page 83

Continued from page 83

4. Using liner, add details with Licorice.

Damselfly:
1. Using round brush, base-coat with a wash of Bluebell.

2. Shade with Slate Blue.

3. Using liner, add details with Licorice.

Butterfly:
1. Outline entire butterfly with Licorice. Let dry.

2. Shade next to body with Lemon Custard. Shade outer edges with Raspberry Wine. Shade body with Wrought Iron.

3. Re-outline butterfly and add details with Licorice.

Frog:
1. Refer to Frog Painting Worksheet on page 90. Base-coat with a wash of three parts Lemon Custard and one part Thicket.

2. Shade with Thicket. Highlight with Warm White. Add tints of Portrait Light and of Lemon Custard.

3. Make markings on frog with Thicket and a bit of Wrought Iron.

4. Reinforce shading with Wrought Iron.

5. Base-coat eye with Licorice. Add highlights of Lemon Custard and Warm White.

Ladybugs:
1. Base-coat with Rose Chiffon.

2. Shade with Raspberry Wine.

3. Using handle end of brush, paint dots and head with Licorice. Highlight with Warm White.

Finish:
1. When dry, apply two or more coats of varnish to pot and saucer.

2. Place saucer right side up on top of upside-down pot. Place glass tabletop on top of saucer.

Saucer Pattern

Enlarge pattern 180%

Gigi's Garden Patio Table Closeup

Iris Painting Worksheet

Base-coat with Bluebell.
Shade with Slate Blue.
Highlight with Warm
White.

Reinforce shading
with indigo. Highlight
with Warm White.

Stipple beard with
Raspberry Wine,
Buttercrunch, and
Lemonade.

Daffodil Painting Worksheet

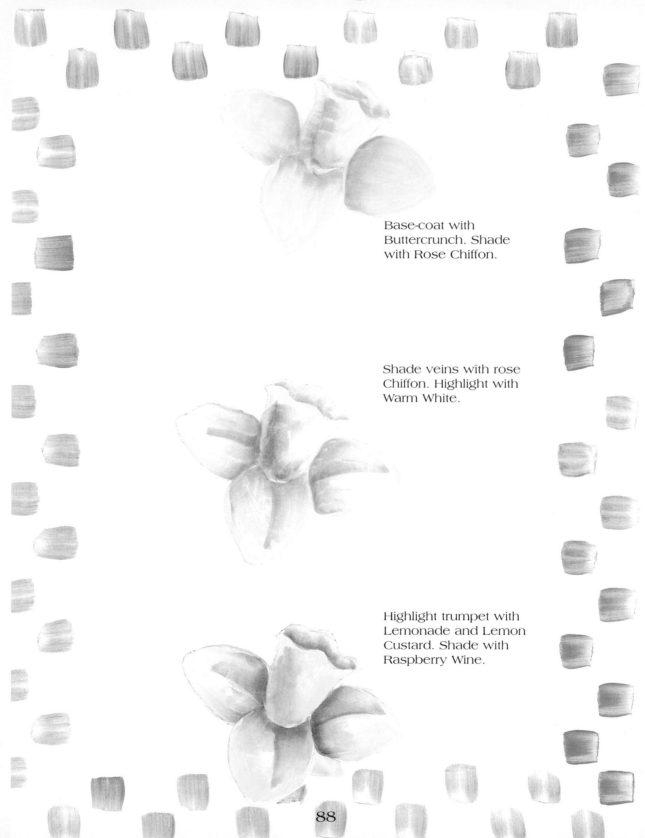

Base-coat with Buttercrunch. Shade with Rose Chiffon.

Shade veins with rose Chiffon. Highlight with Warm White.

Highlight trumpet with Lemonade and Lemon Custard. Shade with Raspberry Wine.

Dragonfly & Damselfly Worksheet

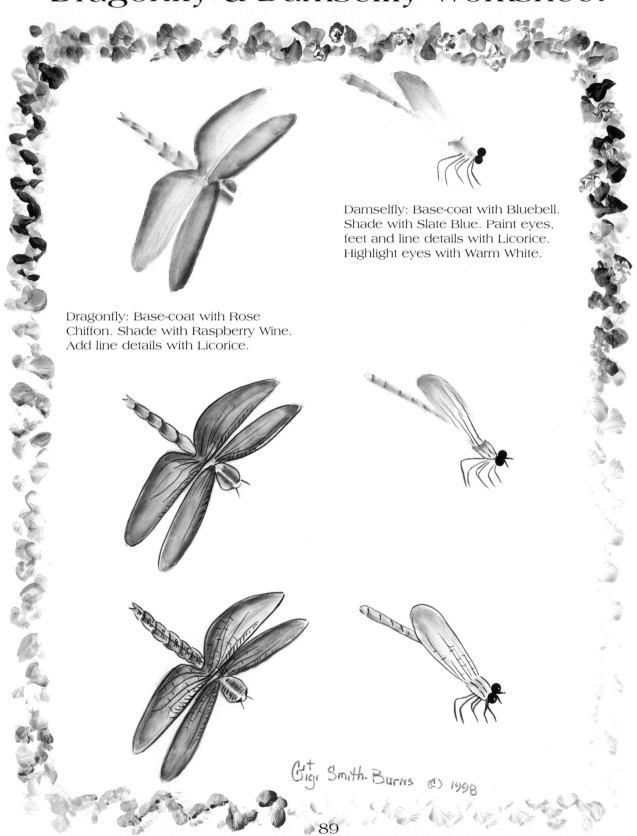

Damselfly: Base-coat with Bluebell.
Shade with Slate Blue. Paint eyes,
feet and line details with Licorice.
Highlight eyes with Warm White.

Dragonfly: Base-coat with Rose
Chiffon. Shade with Raspberry Wine.
Add line details with Licorice.

Gigi Smith-Burns ©) 1998

Frog Painting Worksheet

Body: Base-coat with 3 parts Lemon Custard and 1 part Thicket. Shade with Thicket. Highlight with Warm White. Shade with Wrought Iron.

Eye: Paint eye with Licorice. Shade with Thicket. Highlight with Lemon Custard. Add twinkle with Warm White.

Spots: Paint spots with Thicket and a touch of Wrought Iron.

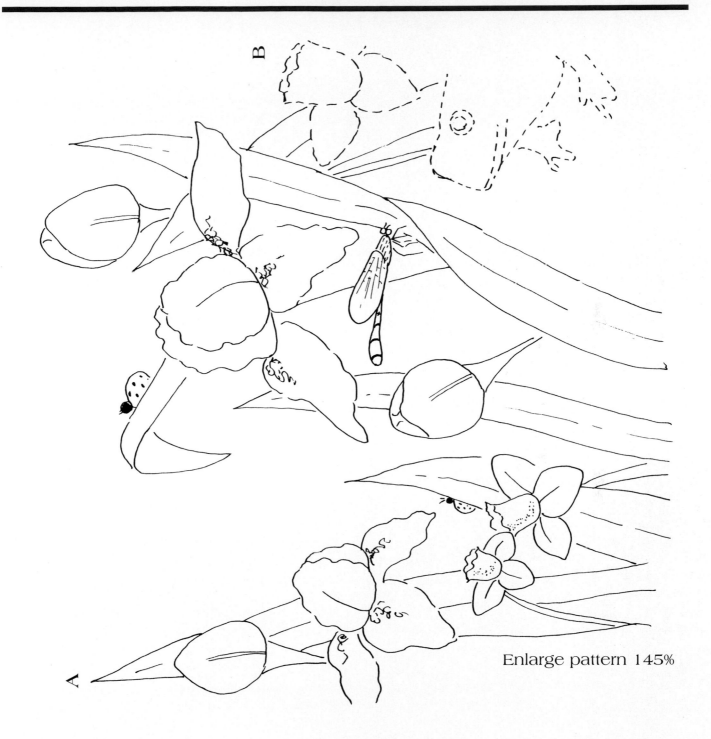

B

A

Enlarge pattern 145%

Pot Pattern #2

C

B

Enlarge pattern 145%

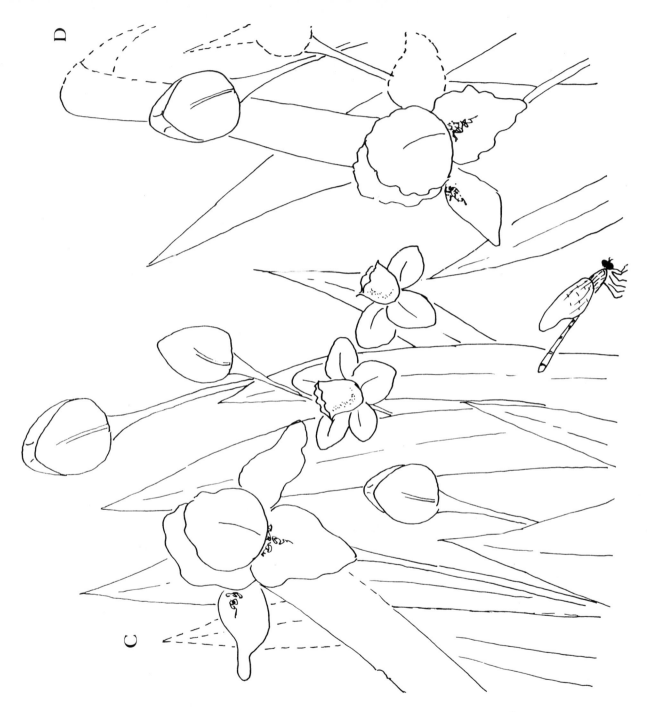

Enlarge pattern 145%

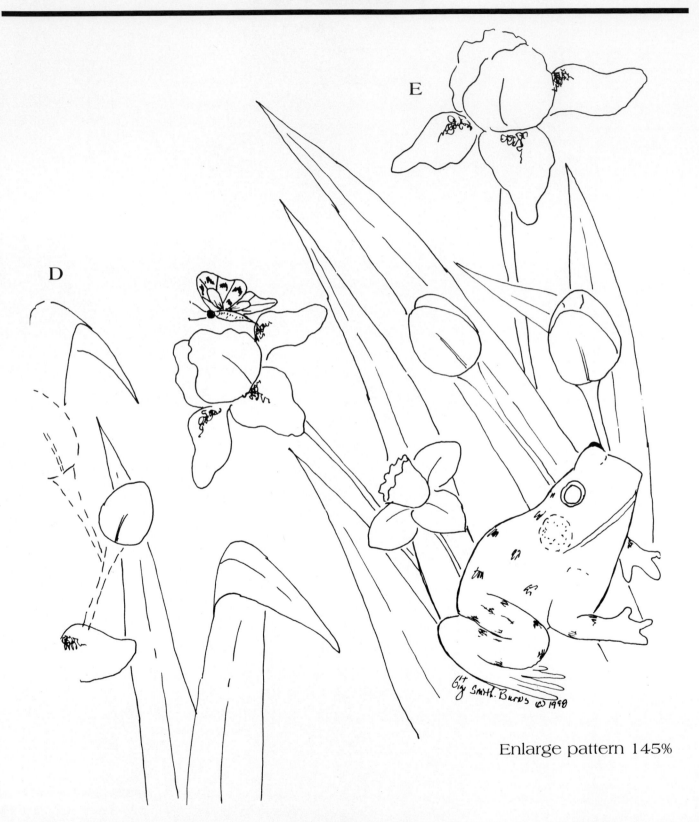

E

D

Guy Smith Burns © 1998

Enlarge pattern 145%

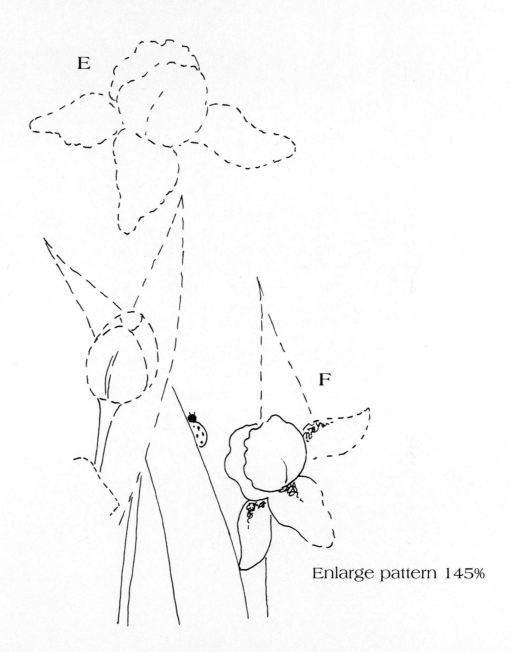

E

F

Enlarge pattern 145%

Pot Pattern #6

Enlarge pattern 145%

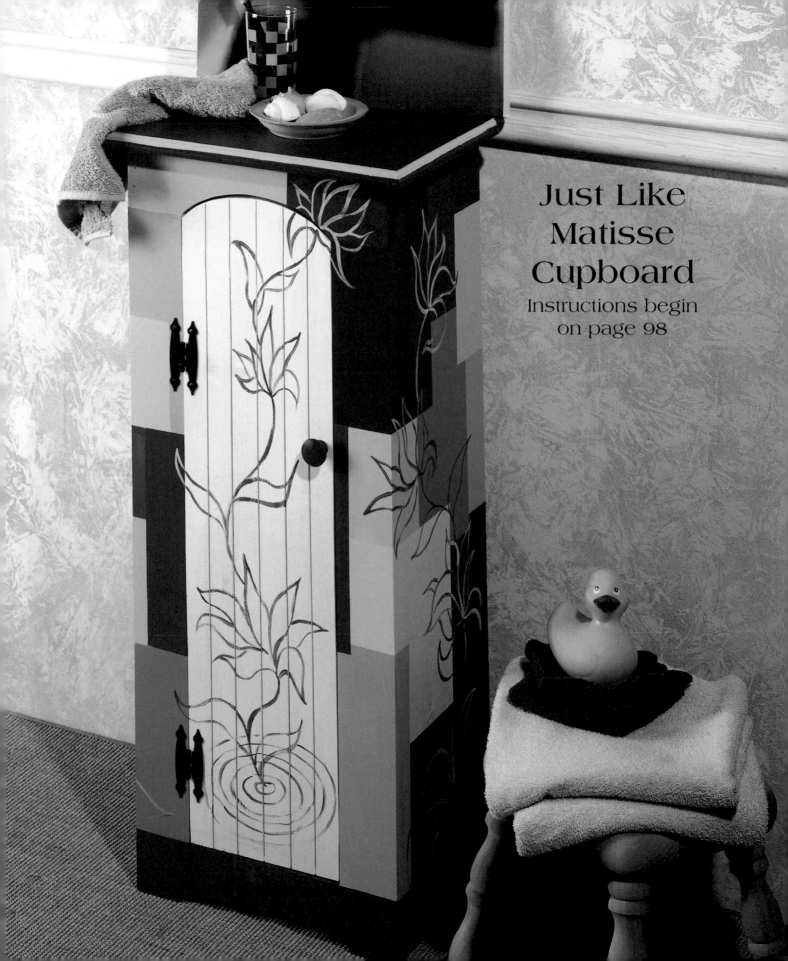

Just Like Matisse Cupboard

Instructions begin
on page 98

Just Like Matisse Cupboard

Pictured on page 97

Designed by
Lisa M. Koo

GATHER THESE SUPPLIES

Painting Surface:
Tall wooden lodge cabinet

Indoor/Outdoor Acrylic Paints:
Antique White
Beachcomber Beige
Dandelion Yellow
Deep Purple
Hot Rod Red
Mossy Green
Spring Green

Brushes:
Round, #5
Sponge brushes, (one per color)

Other Supplies:
Low-tack masking tape
Ruler
Pencil
Transfer tools

INSTRUCTIONS

Prepare:
1. Be certain cabinet is clean and free from dirt and oil. Let dry. Remove hinges and door pull. Referring to Furniture Preparation on pages 6–9, prepare cabinet.

2. Using masking tape, tape off rectangles of different shapes on the sides and front of the cupboard. Using sponge brush, paint rectangles with Beachcomber Beige, Dandelion Yellow, Deep Purple, Hot Rod Red, Mossy Green, and Spring Green. Let dry.

3. Paint door with Antique White. Let dry.

4. Paint top and pull with Hot Rod Red. Let dry.

5. Mask off a stripe ¼"-wide on the rim. Paint stripe on front with Spring Green and on sides with Dandelion Yellow.

Painting the Design:
1. Using transfer tools, transfer Matisse Patterns #1 and #2 on pages 98–99 onto cabinet, referring to photo on page 97 for placement.

Matisse Pattern #1

Enlarge pattern 140%

Matisse Pattern #2

2. Using #5 round brush, paint design elements connecting them with curving vines. Use Mossy Green on door and where design crosses light-colored rectangles on sides. Use Dandelion Yellow where design crosses dark-colored rectangles on sides. Let dry.

Finish:
1. Replace hinges and door pull.

2. No sealing is necessary with indoor/outdoor acrylic paints.

Enlarge patterns 140%

Funky Flowers
Tray Table

Pictured on page 101

Designed by
Holli Long

GATHER THESE SUPPLIES

Painting Surface:
Wooden tray table

Indoor/Outdoor Acrylic Paints:
Antique White
Black
Lanier Blue
Pink Blush
Spring Green

Brushes:
Round, #3
Liner
Sponge brush

Other Supplies:
Low-tack masking tape
Pencil
Ruler
Transfer tools

INSTRUCTIONS

Prepare:
1. Be certain table is clean and free from dirt and oil. Let dry. Referring to Furniture Preparation on pages 6–9, prepare table.

2. Using sponge brush, paint base with Black. Paint lower stretchers and small wooden knobs on insides of legs with Spring Green.

3. Paint sides and bottom of tray with Spring Green. Let dry.

4. Using ruler and pencil, divide bottom of tray into six 7" squares. Mask off ½"-wide lines between squares. Paint lines with Spring Green. Remove tape. Let dry.

5. Mask off three squares and paint with Black. Remove tape. Let dry.

6. Mask off remaining squares and paint one with Lanier Blue, one with Pink Blush, and one with Antique White. Remove tape. Let dry.

Painting the Design:
1. Using transfer tools, transfer Funky Flower Pattern below onto black squares on tray top. Paint flowers, matching the paint color of the flower to its adjacent square, referring to the photo on page 101 for color placement. Let dry.

2. Paint flower centers with Spring Green.

3. Using liner, outline Antique White flower with Pink Blush. Outline Pink Blush flower with Lanier Blue. Outline Lanier Blue flower with Antique White.

4. Paint squiggles around Antique White flower with Lanier Blue. Paint squiggles around Pink Blush flower with Antique White. Paint squiggles around Lanier Blue flower with Pink Blush. Let dry.

Finish:
1. No sealing is necessary with indoor/outdoor acrylic paints.

Funky Flower Pattern

Enlarge pattern 200%

Funky Flowers
Tray Table
Instructions begin
on page 100

Simple Sampler
Chair & Magazine Rack

Pictured on page 103

GATHER THESE SUPPLIES

Painting Surfaces:
Wooden chair
Wooden magazine rack,
    10" x 17½" x 20" high

Acrylic Craft Paints:
Bright Pastel Green
French Blue
Fuchsia
Lavender Sachet
Lemonade
Licorice
Light Periwinkle
Mint Green
Orchid
Wicker White

Brushes:
Sponge brushes

Other Supplies:
Low-tack masking tape, 1"- &
    2"-wide
Matte acrylic sealer
Sponges, small circle, large
    square, medium swirl

INSTRUCTIONS

Prepare:
1. Be certain chair and magazine rack are clean and free from dirt and oil. Let dry. Referring to Furniture Preparation on pages 6–9, prepare chair and magazine rack.

2. Using sponge brush, base-coat chair legs with Bright Pastel Green.

3. Base-coat chair seat and side rungs with French Blue.

4. Base-coat sides of front rung with Licorice.

5. Base-coat back of chair and center bead of front rung with Orchid.

6. Base-coat center beads on front rung with Wicker White.

7. Using 2"-wide masking tape as a guide, base-coat inside magazine rack and around checkerboard areas outside of rack with French Blue.

8. Base-coat vertical rungs of rack sides with Orchid.

9. Base-coat upper horizontal areas of rack sides with Lemonade.

Painting the Design:
Chair:
1. Using 1"-wide masking tape as a guide, paint alternating stripes at lower chair back and front chair apron with Licorice and Wicker White. Let dry.

2. Using swirl sponge, paint swirls on back of chair with Fuchsia. Let dry.

3. Using square sponge, paint half of squares on chair seat in alternating rows the width of sponge with Lavender Sachet. Let dry.

4. Paint other half of squares on chair seat with Light Periwinkle. Let dry.

5. Using circle sponge, paint dots on legs and back supports of chair with Mint Green. Let dry.

Magazine rack:
1. Using 2"-wide masking tape, mask off a checkerboard pattern on top and sides of rack.

2. Paint half of checks with Lemonade and the other half with Orchid. Refer to photo on page 103 for color placement.

Finish:
1. Apply several coats of matte acrylic sealer to chair and magazine rack.

Simple Sampler
Chair & Magazine Rack
Instructions begin on
page 102

Creating Finishes

Creating a Crackled Finish

Preparing the Project:
1. Base-coat the piece. Let dry.

2. Mix crackle medium and acrylic craft paint in equal amounts. Apply generously in areas you wish to crackle. LET DRY OVERNIGHT.

3. Mix water-based varnish and acrylic craft paint in equal amounts and apply a topcoat to the entire piece. Do not brush repeatedly in one place over the crackle/paint base-coated areas or you may soften the crackling. Even if the paint does not appear smooth, leave it alone. Once dry, you can lightly brush another layer of the topcoat mixture over the surface for a more even appearance.

Tips for Crackling
• DO NOT dry paint with a hair dryer when crackling.

• The thicker the topcoat of paint, the larger the cracks. The thinner the topcoat of paint, the smaller the cracks.

• A small amount of water added to topcoat mix will give a fine web of cracking.

• Practice on a test surface before working on your project.

• The weather (humidity or lack of it) may change the results slightly. Low humidity seems to enhance cracking.

Creating a Faux Finish

By using different mitts, a variety of textures can be applied to all types of surfaces.

Sponging mitts are used to create sponged effects. The resulting pattern is a little denser than that achieved with a natural sea sponge.
Start with a light paint color and sponge over with a light or medium shade of glaze. The glaze color should be darker than the paint color.

Ragging mitts are used to give a light, textured look and subtle contrast without the mess of traditional rag-rolling. The effect can be dramatic or subtle depending on the amount of contrast in colors used and the intensity of the colors themselves.

Mopping mitts create a playful, irregular pattern. Using a damp mopping mitt, distribute paint on mitt, then randomly pat mitt on project.
The type of paint used for sponging, ragging or mopping should be slightly transparent and have a longer drying time than regular acrylic paint. This can be achieved by mixing the paint with a glazing medium.

Mama's Flowers Quilt Rack

Pictured on page 107

Designed by
Ginger Edwards

GATHER THESE SUPPLIES

Painting Surface:
Wooden quilt rack

Acrylic Craft Paints:
Acorn Brown
Amish Blue
Burnt Umber
English Mustard
Ivory White
Lemonade
Mystic Green
Raspberry Wine
Rose Pink
Thicket
Thunder Blue
Wicker White
Wintergreen

Brushes:
Flats, #4, #6, #10, #12, #14, 2"
Liners, 1, 10/0
Sponge brush, 1"

Other Supplies:
Crackle medium
Palette or disposable plates
Sandpaper, 220-grit
Tack cloth
Transfer tools
Water-based varnish
Wood sealer

INSTRUCTIONS

Prepare:
1. Be certain quilt rack is clean and free from dirt and oil. Let dry. Referring to Furniture Preparation on pages 6–9, prepare quilt rack.

2. Using sponge brush, base-coat entire piece with mixture of Rose Pink and wood sealer (1:1 ratio). Let dry. Sand lightly. Using a tack cloth, wipe away dust.

3. Refer to Creating a Crackled Finish on page 104. Mix Rose Pink and crackle medium (1:1 ratio) and generously brush onto edges and sides of rack. Let dry overnight.

4. Topcoat entire piece with mixture of Ivory White and varnish (1:1 ratio). Let dry. Lightly brush more mixture over piece, if necessary, to smooth appearance. Let dry.

5. To give worn, used look, sand to expose some bare wood and undercoat of paint in some areas.

6. Using transfer tools, transfer Rose Patterns #1–#3 on pages 106 and 108 onto outer and inner sides of rack.

Painting the Design:
Roses:
1. Refer to Roses Worksheet on page 109 and Painting Roses on page 110. Base-coat with Rose Pink side-loaded into Ivory White to establish rose.

2. Shade with Raspberry Wine. Deepen mixture of Raspberry Wine plus tiny amount of Wintergreen.

3. Highlight with Wicker White and tiny amount of Lemonade.

4. Tint inside throats of flowers with tiny amount of English Mustard.

5. Stipple flower centers with Burnt Umber plus a tiny amount of Raspberry Wine; thin paint with water for softer appearance. Highlight centers with Lemonade plus tiny amount of English Mustard.

6. While painting flowers, add wash of the middle value to drawer pull and rim of heart cutout.

Leaves & Buds:
1. Base-coat all leaves with Amish Blue. Leave some of leaves without further enhancement.

2. Shade some leaves with Thicket. Shade further with Thicket plus small amount of Thunder Blue. You may also add a tiny amount of Wintergreen to mixture, if desired.

3. Tint some leaf edges with English Mustard and Raspberry Wine.

4. Highlight some leaves with Mystic Green and Lemonade. Paint veins on some leaves with this same mix.

5. Paint buds with same colors used for leaves.

Stems & Tendrils:
1. Indicate stems with wash of Burnt Umber. Let dry.

2. Shade with Burnt Umber plus tiny amount of Thunder Blue.

3. Highlight with Ivory White and Acorn Brown.

4. Indicate thorns with Acorn Brown plus tiny amount of Raspberry Wine.

5. Paint tendrils with Thicket plus touch of Thunder Blue.

Finish:
1. After paint is dry, brush a background around the design using any or all of the following colors: Amish Blue, Rose Pink, and Thunder Blue.

2. When dry, protect project with several coats of varnish.

Rose Pattern #1

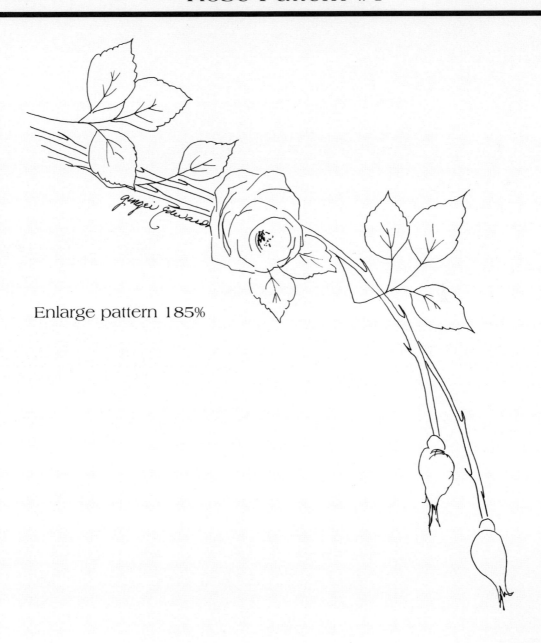

Enlarge pattern 185%

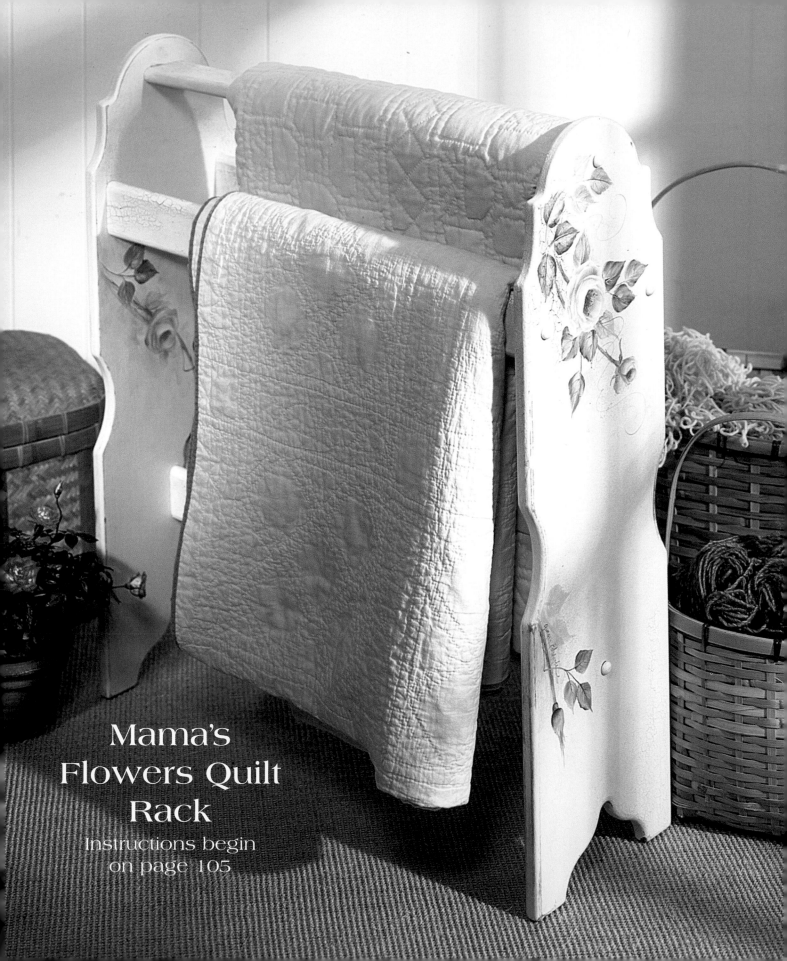

Mama's
Flowers Quilt
Rack

Instructions begin
on page 105

Rose Pattern #2

Enlarge patterns 180%

Rose Pattern #3

Roses Worksheet

Lightly moisten surface with water prior to painting for a softer look and better blending. Establish back and sides of roses. Establish leaves and stems with paint thinned with water to a light value.

Establish center front of cup and outer perimeter. Blend paint so there are no harsh edges of color inside the rose. Shade leaves and stems.

Complete petals. Shade and highlight to complete rose. Deepen shading, high-lighting, and tints. Finish stems. Add a slight background to enhance painting.

Painting Roses

Preparing the Project:
1. Prepare painting surface according to project instructions.

2. Transfer rose design.

Painting the Design:
Rose:
The paint will be easier to stroke and blend over a slightly moist surface. Brush the moisture well beyond the edges of the rose. The surface should have a dull sheen rather than a bright, shiny look. If you have used too much water, you will see the shiny look. Do not blot the area. Simply brush the water further out onto the project surface.

As long as the surface is moist and the paint blends, you can continue to work. Once the paint begins to dry, finish what you are doing, then allow the paint to dry. Brush another film of water over the surface to continue. You may repeat this procedure as often as needed to finish painting the rose. Use a large, flat brush to paint the rose. When painting a rose that is approximately 3" wide, use at least a #16 flat brush. For narrower petals, switch to a smaller flat brush.

1. Brush thin film of water over area where the rose is placed.

2. Load brush with basic color (or mix), then side-load into white. Stroke outermost petals at back of rose. Using dirty brush, side-load into white again and add other petals slightly inside first ones. Make these strokes slightly shorter than previous strokes. Wipe brush and blend lightly.

3. Load brush with basic color, side-load into white, and paint front of bowl of rose. Connect this stroke only on one side to back petals. Reload brush and stroke again, if necessary. Wipe brush and blend.

4. Load brush with basic color, side-load into white, and paint outermost side and lower petals. Several slightly curved strokes will be necessary to completely form outer shape of rose. Reload brush as necessary. Some of these strokes should overlap each other. Wipe brush and blend as necessary.

5. Indicate several petals in the void between center cup or bowl and outer petals to complete rose. Use a smaller flat brush for this. Usually three to five strokes will be needed to amply fill void. Let paint dry before continuing.

6. To add life to rose, lightly moisten rose and use very small amounts of paint to shade, tint, or highlight it.

Procedure:
When painting in small increments, let paint dry between steps, there is no worry that something will be messed up while doing next steps.

1. Moisten surface. Shade and blend. Let dry.

2. Remoisten surface. Add tints and blend. Let dry.

3. Remoisten surface. Lightly brush on additional highlights. Let dry.

4. Paint details (such as centers or veins) without moistening.

Leaves, Stems, Buds & Tendrils:
1. Again, work on slightly moist surface when stroking leaves onto surface. Place all leaves you wish, using paint thinned with water to a light value. Let dry.

2. Moisten surface to allow more time to work with paints, then shade and highlight. Often, some leaves are not enhanced with shading and highlighting.

3. Add stems, buds, and tendrils. Be certain colors remain soft in keeping with rest of painting. Let dry.

Background:
It will enhance painting greatly to add color to the background surrounding the design.

1. Lightly moisten surface with water. With either a flat brush or a large, dry mop brush, lightly brush around design with soft, muted colors. While paint and surface are still wet, blend paints so there are no harsh lines of color.

2. With clean, damp brush, remove any background paint that might have seeped onto roses.

Lady's Writing Desk

Instructions begin
on page 112

Claude Monet *1840-1926*

Lady's Writing Desk

Pictured on page 111

Designed by
Ginger Edwards

GATHER THESE SUPPLIES

Painting Surface:
Old dressing table or desk

Acrylic Craft Paints:
Aspen Green
Basil Green
Buttercrunch
Heather
Ivory White
Lavender Sachet
Lemonade
Mint Green
Night Sky
Periwinkle
Poetry Green
Purple
Raspberry Wine
Raw Sienna
Rose Garden
Sunflower
Wicker White
Wintergreen

Latex Wall Paint:
Pale Butter Yellow

Glazing Mediums:
Black
Deep Woods Green
Neutral
Sage Green

Brushes:
Filberts, #4, #10
Flats, #4, #8, #10, #12, old #4

French brush
Liner, #1
Mop brush
Rounds, #1, #3
Scroller, 10/0

Sponge brushes
Stipple tool

Other Supplies:
Glaze gloss liquid sealer
Low-tack masking tape
New hardware
Palette knife
Palette or disposable plates
Pencil
Ruler
Sandpaper, 220-grit
Sea sponge
Tack cloth
Transfer tools
Water-based varnish

INSTRUCTIONS

Prepare:
1. Be certain table or desk is clean and free from dirt and oil. Let dry. Remove hardware. Referring to Furniture Preparation on pages 6–9, prepare table or desk.

2. Using sponge brush, base-coat sides, drawer fronts, and legs with 1–2 coats Pale Butter Yellow. Let dry. Sand between coats. Using tack cloth, wipe away dust.

3. Base-coat top with Poetry Green. Let dry.

Sponged Panels:
1. Using ruler and pencil, measure and mark panels to receive the sponged finish. Mask off panels.

2. Dip dampened sea sponge in Buttercrunch and press on surface to create texture. Repeat until all areas to be sponged have been covered. Remove tape. Let dry.

3. If furniture piece has turned legs, sponge some areas of the legs. Mask off as needed. Remove tape. Let dry.

4. Mix 3 parts Basil Green with 1 part Aspen Green. Paint a line around each panel. If piece has turned legs, add some lines to the legs as well. Let dry.

5. Using transfer tools, transfer Floral Design Patterns #1 and #2 on pages 115 and 116 onto table or desk, referring to photo on page 111 for placement.

Painting the Design:
Floral Spray:
1. Using #10 flat brush, splotch a muted background behind the floral spray with Raw Sienna plus small amount of Aspen Green that has been thinned with water. Control the intensity of the color with the amount of water used.

2. Using liner, paint weed stems with the watery background mix.

3. Using #4 flat brush, add leaves to stems with the same mixture. Let dry.

Leaves & Stems:
1. Using #8 flat brush, base-coat larger leaves around roses and daisies with Basil Green plus a speck of Aspen Green.

2. Shade with Wintergreen plus a speck of Night Sky.

3. Highlight with Basil Green plus Lemonade.

4. Using #4 flat brush, stroke small leaves on stems on

either side of spray with base-coat mix.

Blue-purple Daisy Petals:
1. Using #3 round brush, base-coat petals with Periwinkle.

2. Using #4 flat brush, shade with Night Sky.

3. Using #3 round brush, highlight with Lavender Sachet plus tiny amount of Periwinkle. Paint brightest highlights with highlight mix plus Wicker White.

Red-purple Daisy Petals:
1. Using #4 flat brush, base-coat red-purple daisy petals with Heather. Shade with Purple.

2. Using #3 round brush, highlight with Wicker White plus tiny amount of Heather. Paint brightest highlights with highlight mix and Wicker White.

Daisy Centers:
1. Using #4 flat brush, base-coat with Sunflower. Shade with Raw Sienna. Deepen shading with Raw Sienna plus tiny amount of Raspberry Wine.

2. Using stipple tool, stipple highlights with Lemonade.

Bleeding Hearts:
The bleeding hearts are the flowers hanging from stems on either side of the spray.

1. Load #4 filbert with Rose Garden, side-load with Ivory White, and paint a single comma stroke for each flower.

2. Using #1 round brush, side-

Side Drawers

load with Rose Garden and small amount of Raspberry Wine. Shade one side of each flower.

3. Side-load #1 round brush with Ivory White and tiny amount of Rose Garden and highlight opposite side of each flower.

4. Using handle end of brush, connect flowers to stems with

dots of Aspen Green. Each dot represents the calyx of a flower.

Roses:
1. Base-coat with Rose Garden.

2. Shade with Rose Garden plus Raspberry Wine.

3. Highlight with Ivory White plus a small amount of Rose

Garden. Add strongest high-lights with Wicker White plus a speck of Rose Garden.

4. Using handle end of brush, add dots in the centers of the roses with Lemonade.

Marbleize the Top:

Refer to Creating a Faux Finish on page 104. To keep faux-marble finish from detracting from painted design, keep colors close in value. Allow each step to dry before continuing.

1. Using French brush, apply Poetry Green to one area of top. Next to that apply Mint Green. With a stippling motion, blend colors with French brush. Work in small areas until surface is covered. Be certain to apply colors to edges of top as well. Let dry.

2. Using a palette knife, mix 3 parts Deep Woods Green, 3 parts Sage Green, and 1 part Black. Mix Neutral with a small amount of water.

3. Using French brush, brush a thin film of diluted Neutral glaze over 12"–14" area.

4. Using old #4 flat brush, stipple with green glaze mixture. The underpainting will show through. Continue moistening surface and stippling glaze until top and edges are covered.

5. Using mop brush to blend, lightly brush surface.

6. Thin some green glaze mixture greatly with water. Using scroller, add veins

extending from darker stippled areas.

7. Using mop brush, lightly blend veins. Let dry.

8. Evaluate look of faux marble. Add more stippling or veins as desired.

9. Thin some green glaze mixture with equal amounts of water and Neutral and apply a final transparent wash to entire top. Let dry thoroughly.

Finish:

1. Brush several coats of gloss liquid sealer on top. Option: Use varnish for final coat if you do not like a high-gloss finish.

2. Apply at least two coats varnish to the remainder of desk. Let dry.

3. Option: Wax and buff piece for added sheen.

4. Install any hardware.

Floral Design Patterns #1

Top of Sponged Panel

Center Front Apron

Narrow Apron on Desk Bottom

Center Front Apron

Small Drawers

Center Front Apron

Enlarge patterns 150%

Large Drawers & Recessed Panels

Sponged Panel Corners

Enlarge patterns 150%

Little
Kids'
Furniture

Instructions
begin on
page 118

Little Kids' Furniture

Nothing is sweeter than a child's laugh and giggle. This design reflects the happiness of childhood and we know this painted set would bring a smile to the face of any child.

Creative Tips

• Think in shapes. A head is a round ball, arms and legs are sticks with things at the ends, hands are little sticks that meet at a palm, and sneakers go at the ends of the legs and are simply "L's" with a thick white underline.

• Clothes are easy, too. T-shirts are squares with little squares attached for sleeves. A dress is a triangle with its tip cut off and squares attached for sleeves. Pants are two stripes of various widths that meet at the crotch. Shorts are the same but shorter, and spandex pants are the same but thinner.

• Hairdos: A lot of boys, and girls for that matter, do not have much hair these days. Tiny lines across the top of a head will make a great flattop. A ponytail is a leaf coming out from a head, then just add some bangs. Dreadlocks are made easily with a small, stiff, dry brush; add bits of color to them for beads.

• Smiles are big. Eyes are little.

• Accessories are limitless and important. Just a few are glasses, earrings, watches, and scrunchies.

• A #1 liner is perfect for detailing and lettering. Use inky paint.

• Balloons are polka dots of color that are outlined with a permanent fine-point marker; also add ends and strings.

• Skin Colors: I used three different colors so that I would have kids of many shades.

Coat Tree of Many Colors

Designed by
Allison Stilwell

Pictured on page 119

GATHER THESE SUPPLIES

Painting Surface:
Unfinished wooden child's coat tree

Acrylic Craft Paints:
Fresh Foliage
Licorice
Light Periwinkle
Purple Lilac
Sunflower
Tangerine
Turquoise
Warm White

Brushes:
Flat, #12

Other Supplies:
Matte acrylic sealer

INSTRUCTIONS

Prepare:
1. Be certain coat tree is clean and free from dirt and oil. Let dry. Referring to Furniture Preparation on pages 6–9, prepare coat tree.

Paint the Design:
1. Using #12 flat brush, paint each side of the coat tree a different color with Fresh Foliage, Purple Lilac, Sunflower, and Turquoise.

2. Paint top of first base support with Sunflower; sides with Tangerine and Turquoise.

3. Paint top of second base support with Light Periwinkle; sides with Sunflower.

4. Paint top of third base support with Purple Lilac; sides with Licorice.

5. Paint top of fourth base support with Tangerine; sides with Fresh Foliage and Purple Lilac.

6. Paint hooks with Licorice.

7. Add Warm White polka dots to all Licorice surfaces.

Finish:
1. Apply matte acrylic sealer to coat tree.

Coat Tree of
Many Colors

Instructions begin
on page 118

Laughs Table & Giggles Chair

Designed by
Allison Stilwell

Pictured on pages 121 & 123

GATHER THESE SUPPLIES

Painting Surfaces:
Unfinished wooden table &
   chairs for children

Acrylic Craft Paints:
Azure Blue
Buttercup
Glazed Carrots
Licorice
Light Blue
Light Periwinkle
Lilac
Lime Light
Medium Orange
Orchid
Patina
Purple Lilac
Sunflower
Tangerine
Teddy Bear Tan
Turquoise
Warm White

Brushes:
Flats, 1", #12
Liner, #1

Other Supplies:
Black permanent fine-point
   marker
Matte acrylic sealer
Transfer tools

INSTRUCTIONS

Prepare Table:
1. Be certain table and chairs
are clean and free from dirt
and oil. Let dry. Referring to
Furniture Preparation on pages
6–9, prepare table and chairs.

2. Using #12 flat brush, base-
coat tabletop with Buttercup.

3. Base-coat rim of tabletop
with Glazed Carrots and
Medium Orange. Let dry.

4. Using 1" flat brush, add checks
around rim with Tangerine.

5. Base-coat short sides with
Sunflower.

6. Base-coat one long side
with Turquoise and other long
side with Lime Light.

7. Base-coat drawers with
Tangerine. Let dry. Paint rims
of drawers with Licorice.

8. Base-coat each leg a different color—Lilac, Lime Light,
Orchid, Patina.

9. Using transfer tools and the
Laughs & Giggles Patterns on
page 124, transfer the word
"Laughs" onto one drawer and
the word "Giggles" onto other
drawer. Transfer children onto
tabletop.

Paint Table Design:
1. Using #1 liner, paint lettering
on drawers with Licorice.

2. Referring to Creative Tips on
page 118, dress kids.

3. Use different colors to add
¾" polka dots to the Sunflower
sides of table. When dry, turn
polka dots into balloons by
adding ends and strings with
permanent fine-point marker.

4. Add Warm White polka dots
to Licorice rims.

Prepare Giggles Chair:
1. Using #12 flat brush, base-

coat both sides of chair back
with Purple Lilac. Paint rim of
chair back with Licorice.

2. Base-coat chair seat with
Light Periwinkle. Paint seat
rims with Patina. Base-coat
front support with Sunflower.

3. Base-coat outside of left leg
with Lime Light and inside
with Patina. Paint front rim with
Orchid and back rim with Light
Periwinkle. Paint rounded
lower rim with Azure Blue.

4. Base-coat outside of right
leg with Tangerine and inside
with Light Blue. Paint front rim
with Licorice and back rim
with Patina. Paint rounded
lower rim with Azure Blue.

5. Transfer children from the
Laughs & Giggles Patterns on
page 124 onto center top front
of chair backs. Transfer two
children to the front of each
chair back.

Paint Giggles Chair:
1. Using #1 liner, paint lettering
with Licorice.

2. Referring to Creative Tips on
page 118, dress kids.

3. Add different colors of ¾"
polka dots to Sunflower front
support. When polka dots
have dried, turn them into
balloons by outlining with a
permanent fine-point marker
and adding ends and strings.

4. Add Warm White polka dots
to Licorice rims.

Prepare Laughs Chair:
1. Using #12 flat brush, base-
coat both sides of chair back
Continued on page 122

Laughs Table
Instructions begin
on page 120

Instructions begin
on page 120

Continued from page 120

with Light Periwinkle. Paint rim of chair back with Licorice.

2. Base-coat chair seat with Purple Lilac. Paint rims of seat with Medium Orange. Base-coat front support with Purple Lilac.

3. Base-coat outside of left leg with Patina and inside with Orchid. Paint front rim with Licorice and back rim with Light Periwinkle. Paint rounded lower rim with Azure Blue.

4. Base-coat outside of right leg with Sunflower and inside with Lime Yellow. Paint front rim with Patina and back rim with Licorice. Paint rounded lower rim with Azure Blue.

5. Transfer children from the Laughs & Giggles Patterns on page 124 onto center top front of chair back. Transfer two kids to front of chair back.

Paint Laughs Chair:
1. Using #1 liner, paint lettering with Licorice.

2. Referring to Creative Tips on page 118, dress kids.

3. Add Warm White polka dots to Licorice rims.

4. Add different colors of ¾" polka dots to outside of right Sunflower chair leg. When polka dots have dried, turn them into balloons by outlining with permanent fine-point marker and adding ends and strings.

Finish:
1. Apply matte acrylic sealer to table and chairs.

Giggles Bench

Pictured on page 125

GATHER THESE SUPPLIES

Painting Surface:
Unfinished wooden bench

Acrylic Craft Paints:
Fresh Foliage
Licorice
Light Periwinkle
Medium Yellow
Patina
Purple Lilac
Sunflower
Tangerine

Latex Wall Paint:
Warm White

Brushes:
Flat, #12
Liner, #1

Other Supplies:
Black permanent fine-point marker
Transfer tools

INSTRUCTIONS

Prepare:
1. Be certain bench is clean and free from dirt and oil. Let dry. Referring to Furniture Preparation on pages 6–9, prepare bench.

2. Using #12 flat brush, base-coat bench with Warm White. Let dry.

3. Paint top surface with Fresh Foliage. Paint rim on a short side with Licorice and on other short side with Light Periwinkle. Paint rim on one long side with Sunflower and the other long side with Tangerine.

4. Paint center support with Patina. Paint top rim of center support with Tangerine. Paint ends of support, which extend on outside of legs, with Tangerine. Paint braces, which go through support ends, with Fresh Foliage.

5. Paint outside right leg with Purple Lilac and inside with Light Periwinkle. Paint front rim with Licorice and back rim with Sunflower.

6. Paint outside left leg with Medium Yellow and inside with Sunflower. Paint front rim with Sunflower and back rim with Licorice.

7. Paint lower curved rim of each leg with Purple Lilac.

8. Using transfer tools, transfer Laughs & Giggles Patterns on page 124 onto bench center. Transfer a kid to each side of lettering.

Paint the Design:
1. Using #1 liner, paint lettering with Licorice.

2. Referring to Creative Tips on page 118, dress kids.

3. Add different colors of ¾" polka dots to inside of leg painted with Sunflower. When polka dots have dried, turn them into balloons by outlining with a permanent fine-point marker and adding ends and strings.

4. Add Warm White polka dots to Licorice rims.

Finish:
1. Apply matte acrylic sealer to bench.

Giggles Chair
Instructions begin
on page 120

Laughs and Giggles

Enlarge patterns 230%

Giggles Bench
Instructions begin
on page 122

Product Source

FolkArt® Paints referred to as Acrylic Craft Paints in this book:
Acorn Brown #941
Amish Blue #715
Apple Spice #951
Aspen Green #646
Baby Blue #442
Basil Green #645
Bayberry #922
Blue Ribbon #719
Bluebell #909
Bright Pastel Green #466
Buttercrunch #737
Clay Bisque #601
English Mustard #959
French Blue #639
Fresh Foliage #954
Fuchsia #635
Glazed Carrots #741
Heather #933
Huckleberry #745
Indigo #908
Ivory White #427
Lavender Sachet #625
Lemon Custard #735
Lemonade #904
Licorice #938
Light Blue #402
Light Periwinkle #640
Lime Light #470
Lime Yellow #478
Linen #420
Medium Orange #684
Midnight #964
Mint Green #445
Mystic Green #723
Navy Blue #403
Night Sky #443
Nutmeg #944
Olive Green #449
Orchid #637
Parchment #450
Patina #444
Periwinkle #404
Poetry Green #619
Portrait Light #421
Purple #411
Purple Lilac #439
Raspberry Wine #935
Rose Chiffon #753
Rose Garden #754

Rose Pink #632
Skintone #949
Slate Blue #910
Southern Pine #730
Sunflower #432
Tangerine #627
Tapioca #903
Teal Green #733
Teddy Bear Tan #419
Thicket #924
Thunder Blue #609
Turquoise #961
Wicker White #901
Wintergreen #962
Wrought Iron #925

FolkArt® Artists' Pigments™ referred to as Acrylic Craft Colors in this book:
Burnt Carmine #686
Burnt Sienna #943
Burnt Umber #462
Hauser Green Dark #461
Hauser Green Light #459
Ice Blue #457
Light Red Oxide #914
Medium Yellow #455
Napthol Crimson #435
Pure Orange #628
Raw Sienna #452
Raw Umber #485
Titanium White #480
True Burgundy #456
Warm White #649
Yellow Light #918

FolkArt® Metallic Acrylic Colors:
Pure Gold #660

FolkArt® Products:
Blending Gel Medium
Crackle Medium
Extender
Floating Medium
Glass & Tile Medium
Glazing Medium
Thickener

Antiquing Mediums:
Apple Butter Brown #819

Down Home Brown #812
Woodn' Bucket Brown #817

Finishes:
Artist Varnishes
    Gloss #882
    Satin #885
    Matte #888
Clearcote™ Acrylic Sealer #789
Waterbase Varnish #791

Applicators & Tools:
Brush Plus® Water-base Cleaner/Conditioner #20480

Apple Barrel® Gloss Enamels referred to as Indoor/Outdoor Acrylic Paints in this book:
Beachcomber Beige #20663
Black #20662
Dandelion Yellow #20646
Deep Purple #20625
Eggshell #20622
Hot Rod Red #20637
Lanier Blue #20656
Mossy Green #20648
Pink Blush #20631
Pinwheel Blue #20657
Spring Green #20652
White #20621

Stencil Décor® Dry Brush™ Stencil Paints:
Terra Cotta #26240
Truffles Brown #26206

Stencil Gels:
Berry Red #26111
Blue Blazer #26118
Dark Sapphire #26115
Fern #26123
Ivory Lace #26102
Juniper #26124
King's Gold #26132
Russet #26129
Tempest Blue #26117
Twig #26128

Wedgwood Blue #26116
White #26101
Wild Ivy #26126
Wood Rose #26110

Blender #29206
Stencil Roller #34006
Spouncer™ ¾" #1533, 1¼" #1534, 1¾" #1535
Daubers ⅜" #50137, ¼" #50138

Brush Cleaner & Bristle Scrubber #26251
Stencil Blank #26667

Laser-cut Borders:
Oak Leaves #27713

Multilayer Borders:
Blooming Rose #26737
Canterbury Scroll #26648
Magnolia Blossoms #26709

Elements for Murals:
Bricks & Cobblestones #26855
Pots & Planters #26854
Window #26856

Simply® Stencils:
Checkerboard Collection #28771
Spring Vines #28368

Stamp Décor™ Stamps:
Leaf Collection #53661
Martha's Fern #53610
Medallion Collection #53662

Glaze Applicators #53477
Glaze Roller #53476
Stamp Cleaner #53478

Decorator Blocks™:
Critters #53220
Dandelion & Italian Foxgloves #53239
Geraniums #53210

Geraniums #53210
Hollyhocks #53240
Iris/Daffodils #53215
Ivy #53202
Lilac & Hydrangeas
 #53217
Parsley #53262
Sage, Mint, Chives #53263
Tulips #53213

Decorator Glazes
referred to as Glazing
Mediums in this book:
Alpine Green #53044
Bark Brown #53033
Black #53034

Deep Purple #53020
Deep Woods Green
 #53032
Geranium Red #53012
Italian Sage #53045
Ivy Green #53031
Lemon Yellow #53007
Lilac #53022
Moss Green #53043
Mushroom #53049
Nantucket Navy #53025
Neutral #53001
New Gold Leaf #53002
New Leaf Green #53029
Olde World Bronze #53004
Pompeii Red #53038

Sage Green #53028
Sky Blue #53026

Durable Colors™ referred
to as Indoor/Outdoor
Acrylic Paints in this
book:
Damask Blue #53314
Vanilla #53302
White #53301

Decorator Sealers:
Gloss # 30141
Matte #30142

Brush Set #53453
French Brush #30122
Mopping Mitt #30107
Mopping Tool #30129
Ragging Mitt #30106
Sea Sponge #31050
Sea Sponge Mitt #30108
Spatter Tool #30121
Sponge Mitt #30105

Fun to Paint™ Products:
Circles #50118
Squares #50119
Swirls #50125

Metric Conversion Chart

MM-Millimetres   CM-Centimetres

INCHES TO MILLIMETRES AND CENTIMETRES

INCHES	MM	CM	INCHES	CM	INCHES	CM
⅛	3	0.3	9	22.9	30	76.2
¼	6	0.6	10	25.4	31	78.7
½	13	1.3	12	30.5	33	83.8
⅝	16	1.6	13	33.0	34	86.4
¾	19	1.9	14	35.6	35	88.9
⅞	22	2.2	15	38.1	36	91.4
1	25	2.5	16	40.6	37	94.0
1¼	32	3.2	17	43.2	38	96.5
1½	38	3.8	18	45.7	39	99.1
1¾	44	4.4	19	48.3	40	101.6
2	51	5.1	20	50.8	41	104.1
2½	64	6.4	21	53.3	42	106.7
3	76	7.6	22	55.9	43	109.2
3½	89	8.9	23	58.4	44	111.8
4	102	10.2	24	61.0	45	114.3
4½	114	11.4	25	63.5	46	116.8
5	127	12.7	26	66.0	47	119.4
6	152	15.2	27	68.6	48	121.9
7	178	17.8	28	71.1	49	124.5
8	203	20.3	29	73.7	50	127.0

Index